HUNTLEY MEADOWS

A Natural Treasure

Rodney Fisher

Printed in the United States of America
ISBN: 978-1-7370501-0-0 Softcover
ISBN: 978-1-7370501-1-7 Ebook

Library of Congress Control Number: 2021907406
Photography and Text by Rodney Fisher
Editing by Alice Heiserman
Graphics Design by Xavaire Bolton

Contents

Chapter 1. Introduction

"Wetlands may not have the grandeur of towering mountain ranges, but they still rank among the most spectacular and impressive of the Earth's ecosystems." ~ Peter D. Moore

If Hybla Valley in Alexandria, Virginia, had been developed, instead of evolving into our idyllic Huntley Meadows, our world might feel quite different. The Lockheed Boulevard Connector, with Route 1, would likely groan under the weight of unrelenting traffic. Residential and commercial development might have spread out through what is currently the woods. Perhaps a strip mall anchored by a gas station and convenience store would fill the current wetlands. Life with all of its noise and intensity would seem to crowd out our ability to escape. And most unfortunately, those desiring a safe and beautiful space nearby, would be forced to go elsewhere. But that is not our story.

Established in 1975, Huntley Meadows has blossomed into healthy forest, freshwater wetlands, and meadows. This 1,500-acre jewel in the Fairfax County park system, blocks from a major national highway, is a renowned flyway and animal reserve.[1] The park exists harmoniously with the dense urban sprawl of the Washington, D.C. suburbs. To the delight of 200,000 annual visitors, Huntley Meadows provides serene open space, abundant wildlife, and importantly, peace.[2] The park's wetlands, protected by woods, is invaluable not only for the wildlife it sustains, but also for how it constantly regenerates and transforms the world around it.[3]

Huntley Meadows is a treat for anyone seeking wildness in a dynamic urban area. It is one of the countless surprises one enjoys in Virginia, a state of exceptional beauty and variety. It is the largest of Fairfax County's network of parks. Rich in natural resources, the county is home to 427 parks spread out through 23,000 acres of land, with 325 miles of trails.[4]

Fairfax County, home of Huntley Meadows, was established in 1741 and named after the prominent Fairfax family of Yorkshire, England. In 1719, Thomas Baron Cameron, sixth Lord Fairfax, inherited control of a five million acre land grant between Virginia's Rappahannock and

Potomac Rivers. Fairfax became a friend, neighbor, and mentor to the young George Washington. They built a friendship that lasted throughout their lives.[5]

In the modern era, this 391 square-mile county has grown into an economic power-house.[6] With a population of over one million residents, the economy is driven by thousands of dynamic businesses and nonprofits, including ten Fortune 500 firms.[7] Companies here employ one of the younger and most diverse workforces in the nation.[8] In Fairfax County, one of the wealthiest counties in the nation, over 60 percent of residents 25 and older have earned a bachelor's degree or higher, significantly above the national average of 37 percent.[9,10]

Two of the county's exceptional residents include the nation's first President, George Washington, and fellow founding father, George Mason, a signer of the Declaration of Independence and the author of the Virginia Declaration of Rights.[11,12] Adopted in 1776, Mason's Declaration of Rights became a blueprint for the United States Constitution's Bill of Rights, that established rights and civil liberties for American citizens.[13]

This region is a most desirable location to work and live, and parcels of land carry impressive value that rise year after year.[14] Demands of nonstop population growth, however, will continue to entice some to cast envious eyes toward this delicate habitat. For that reason, future generations must vigilantly guard Huntley Meadows' integrity.

Today, classes, walks, tours, lectures, and family friendly events fill the park's calendar. Participatory programs and classes include Owl Outings, Corn Grinding, and Clay Pottery Demonstrations, Kids Nature Journaling, Wilderness Survival Skills, Birding for Beginners, Nature for Tiny Tots, and Catch a Critter, to name a few.[15]

John Muir, the renowned conservationist, wrote, In every walk with nature we receive far more than we seek.[16] Each visit to this park confirms that sentiment for me, because each experience offers a new perspective, view, or surprise. I leave the park inspired. In the "Artist's Introduction" to *The Illuminated Walden*, photographer John Wawrzonek posits that the expectation of seeing something wonderful is necessary to unlock its magic.[17] One can be certain of seeing wild and beautiful things in a constantly changing Huntley Meadows.

With each new season, Huntley Meadows becomes alive with a renewed energy. Steady northwest winds kick in, obscuring the surrounding noise. For a glorious moment, no jets are overhead and not a person is in sight. Countless frogs and birds have become unusually loud, shrill even. I feel vulnerable, as well as joyfully connected to this world. Except for the modern boardwalk, I can imagine that I am in ancient Huntley Meadows as it might have been thousands of years ago.

When darkness descends, I imagine indigenous Indian families celebrating a long day with a feast, complete with singing, dancing, and telling of tales. As much as I want to remain, home beckons. The more I visit, the more I often imagine the evolution of this sacred space. It has been, in some important ways, restored. I hope that you enjoy the following history and photographs. I encourage area residents, as well as visitors, to plan a visit to Huntley Meadows. This park will delight, as well as edify.

Chapter 2. The Virginia Indians

Virginia Indians left no written accounts of their history or culture. The diaries of English settlers provide the only information available to us.[1] These diaries provide us a glimpse into the fascinating new world and people they discovered. Population estimates for Virginia Indians living along the coastal plain in the seventeenth century vary widely from 20,000 to as many as 50,000.[2]

Early European visitors, including Captain John Smith, noted many indigenous communities along the Potomac River, of which the Powhatans and Piscataways were the dominant groups.[3] Northern Virginia Indians were Algonquian-speaking people who were riverene horticulturist or skilled farmers, who also hunted, fished, and foraged for their sustenance.[4] Both men and women cooperated in performing demanding tasks in their respective roles as hunters and food preparers.[5]

Unfortunately, we know little about the Algonquin-speaking Dogue Indians, who lived and hunted in present-day southern Fairfax County. Fish from the nearby Potomac River and its tributaries provided sustenance, while clay from the riverbeds provided material for pottery.[6] An eight-mile tributary of the Potomac River that runs from Mount Vernon, through Huntley Meadows, is named for the Dogue tribe.[7]

Approximately 8,000 years ago, this land was shaped, in large part, by the end of the Ice Age, which resulted in increased rains and flooding of rivers such as the Potomac, depositing rich topsoil on the surrounding plains.[8] As the Southern-Mid-Atlantic climate moderated, it began to provide longer, productive growing seasons. By the time of European colonization, Virginia Indians had large fields under cultivation growing corn, beans, and squash.[9]

Some early Virginia explorers noted the existence of large fields like these under cultivation, and in some locations, observers saw elevated lookouts for designated watchers to frighten away birds and other wildlife.[10]

Early explorers found that good food was plentiful. On his trip along the Potomac and Anacostia Rivers in 1608, Captain Smith recorded that an "Abundance of fish, lying so thicke with their heads above the water, as for want of nets (our barge driving amongst them) we attempted to catch them with a frying pan: but we found it a bad instrument to catch fish with: neither better fish, more plenty, nor more variety for final fish, had any of us ever seene in any place so swimming in the water."[11]

As European colonists expanded their settlements and displaced numerous indigenous communities, Indian and Anglo relations deteriorated. It is likely that the Indians left some areas and joined with other groups.[12]

Chapter 3. The Nineteenth Century —
Historic Huntley Manor

North of Huntley Meadows rests Huntley Manor, a nineteenth century federal-style villa with an expansive view of the countryside.[1] It is part of the property originally purchased in 1757 by George Mason IV, one of the nation's founding fathers, a signatory of the Declaration of Independence, and the author of Virginia's Declaration of Rights, and the Virginia Constitution.[2] The house is considered highly refined for a secondary house of a planter's family of this period.[3]

The property was part of Mason's extensive land holdings, and although his records were lost, he may have once owned as much as 100,000 acres of land.[4] Many prominent colonial planters actively expanded their estates and made considerable effort to ensure their purchases included clear and unclouded (without an outstanding claim) titles. Because boundaries were not firmly established in legal precedent as they are today, some landholders like Mason found it advantageous to become proficient at surveying to protect their property.[5]

In 1769, George Washington and George Mason, colleagues as well as neighbors, surveyed the land that is now in Hybla Valley and separated their adjacent parcels with a 30-foot ditch.[6] Washington's property bordered, but did not extend into what is now Huntley Meadows.[7]

Huntley Manor was constructed around 1825 as a summer retreat by Thomson Francis Mason, a grandson of George Mason IV.[8] Thomson Mason was raised in Hollin Hall, south of Huntley Manor, and after earning his law degree from Princeton University in 1807, returned to Alexandria and became a prominent local attorney. Mason served as mayor of the city (1827-1830 and 1835-1837) and as a member of the Common Council.[9] While it is not known how often the Masons visited the family retreat, he and his family lived nearby in what is now known as Historic Old Town, Alexandria, in the former Colross estate on Oronoco Street.[10]

Ownership of the house changed numerous times, and American Civil War troops used the adjacent property as farmland as well as for a temporary encampment.[11] Following Virginia's secession from the Union, federal troops set up forts throughout the region.[12] During the

Civil War, Union General George McClellan's troops camped on the Huntley Farm in 1862 following the Peninsula Campaign, and before the Battle of Second Manassas.[13] Huntley Manor was eventually abandoned and fell into disrepair. It was rescued in 1989 when the Fairfax County Park Authority acquired the house, restoring it and its surrounding two and one-half acres. Today Historic Huntley is open to the public for tours and educational events from April through October.[14]

Following the Civil War, this rural area of Fairfax County became a flourishing center for crops, livestock, orchards, and dairy production. Dairy alone became the county's largest industry in the mid-1900s, with more than 100 dairy farms.[15]

Historic Huntley is on the National Register of Historic Places, the Virginia Landmarks Register, and the Fairfax County Inventory of Historic Sites.[16] It joins other important local sites to be recognized, including Hollin Hills Historic District, Pohick Episcopal Church, Sydenstricker School (the last one-room schoolhouse in Fairfax County), and the Oakton Trolley Station, among other significant properties.[17]

Chapter 4. The Twentieth Century —
The George Washington Air Junction (1929-1937)

The early twentieth century heralded the birth of aviation. At points both thrilling and dangerous, aircraft evolved and improved from the first private flight in 1903.[1] By 1924 airplanes had successfully traveled coast to coast and around the world. Domestically, they had become important sources of mail delivery. Air shows around the country drew ever-increasing crowds, as pilots entertained with dazzling in-air acrobatics.[2]

Upon discovering that the nation's capital region had yet to establish a major airport,[3] New York aviation enthusiast, Henry Woodhouse, took the initiative in the late 1920s to build his own airport in Northern Virginia. Hybla Valley might have seemed an unlikely place to shape aviation history. Woodhouse, an ambitious man, sought to build a world-renowned air park and found privately owned acres of farmland just south of Washington, D.C. in Hybla Valley, Virginia.[4]

Woodhouse, a former governor of the Aero League of America, was a prolific writer and one of the most consulted aeronautical authorities in the county.[5] He named the proposed airport in Hybla Valley, *the George Washington Air Junction*. The airport plan included two runways of 7,500 and 3,000 feet, respectively, that would have made it the largest in existence, including in Europe.[6] "Our only desire," claimed Woodhouse, "is to solve the problem of supplying to the Capital of this great nation adequate facilities for all developments that may take place in aerial transportation, no matter how extensive."[7]

Woodhouse's plan included building a 300 by 100 foot airplane hangar, establishing an aviation school, and offering aerial tours over historic sites such as Mount Vernon.[8] To draw in the public, he planned to construct a replica of George Washington's childhood schoolhouse, as well as a museum containing Washington's family memorabilia on the grounds.[9]

Woodhouse believed that the air junction was large enough to accommodate transatlantic airplanes, as well as Zeppelins, engine-powered, cigar-shaped, airships, which he felt were the most capable sources for air transportation [10]

Woodhouse succeeded in securing the financial backing to purchase 1,500 acres from 10 local landowners.[11] On February 22, 1929, he pulled off a publicity coup, leading a dedication of the George Washington Air Junction with descendants of President George Washington, as well as public officials, in attendance.[12]

Complicating life, however, was the deepening Great Depression, tightening its vise-like grip on entrepreneurs and creditors alike. Soon Woodhouse's creditors were pursuing him financially and legally, and through a series of defaults, foreclosures, and lawsuits, he lost all of the air junction property.[13] The majority of the proposed air park property, 1,261 acres, was held by the Washington Air Terminals Corporation, which sold it to the federal government in 1941 for $60,000. Thus, Henry Woodhouse inadvertently played a central role in piecing back together the subdivided Hybla Valley farmland that would ultimately become Huntley Meadows Park.[14]

Woodhouse was a most controversial individual, as well as a fraud. Born Mario Terenzio Enrico Casalegno in Turin Italy, Woodhouse reinvented himself after serving a sentence for the murder of a restaurant co-worker. His conviction for murder was discovered later, once he became established. His educational achievement and credentials cannot be verified; yet, he became a prolific and competent writer, quoted by major magazines and newspapers as an aeronautical expert.[15]

Henry Woodhouse became one of the most successful forgers of his time. Finding it a profitable enterprise, he began selling what were supposedly original letters and documents from the family of George Washington.[16] Although authorities never caught or prosecuted Woodhouse, he died in obscurity, his great dream of building a historic air park, unrealized.[17]

Chapter 5. The Era of U.S. Government Use — The Bureau of Public Roads (1944-1954)

The Bureau of Public Roads (BPR), the predecessor of the Federal Highway Administration, was the first federal governmental agency to use the property in Hybla Valley. From 1944 to 1954, the BPR conducted tests at this location on surface road materials.[1] Hybla Valley was a part of a national network of surface-transportation-research sites with nearby McLean, Virginia, serving as the national research center.[2] The BPR research studies, conducted with the help of a 2,000 foot oval track, were coordinated with the Asphalt Institute and the Highway Research Board.[3]

Ensuring safe and durable materials for the rapid growth in needed transportation infrastructure, both locally and nationwide, was a priority for the BPR. The Bureau of Public Road's work included research on pavement temperature and stability when exposed to wind, precipitation, and solar radiation.[4] Testing also focused on the load-carrying capacity of pavement samples, and sub-surface materials, such as soil clays and assessing their suitability as subgrade constituent material for highway subsurfaces.[5,6]

The population growth and mobility of American citizens required the need for ongoing research and development. The population growth in the Commonwealth of Virginia in the twentieth century was surging, and the increased demand for automobiles created a nonstop need for new public roads. In Virginia, motor vehicle registrations rose from 2,705 in 1910 to 983,561 in 1950.[7] In generally the same period, Virginia highways expanded from 4,002 miles in 1918 to 50,359 in 1950.[8]

World War II created challenges domestically, as the federal government diverted road building and maintenance resources to the war effort.[9] In the winter of 1945 and 1946, thousands of miles of Virginia roads crumbled, their repair compounded by a shortage of labor, equipment, and materials.[10] In response, Virginia policymakers implemented a 20-year plan to upgrade roads throughout the state.[11]

By 1950, the population of the United States became predominantly metropolitan for the first time, increasing from 76 million in 1900 to 151 million in 1950.[12,13] The growth of Fairfax County was equally impressive. It took 140 years (1790-1930) for the population of Fairfax County to double, from 12,300 to 25,000 residents. From 1930 to 1950, the population had nearly quadrupled from 25,000 to almost 99,000. Fairfax County's population has since increased to more than 10 times that of 1950, a growth rate rivaling that of any community in the nation.[14]

The Bureau of Public Roads declared the Hybla Valley land surplus property, as it began to conduct its research on roads that were currently in use. The Department of Defense then secured the land to serve as a proving ground for Army and Navy equipment.[15]

Chapter 6. The Cold War Years —
The National Guard Anti-aircraft Station (1951-1957)

From 1951 to 1957, Hybla Valley played a role in the country's national security during some of the twentieth century's tense Cold War years. During this period, the Virginia National Guard's Battery D, 125th Gun Battalion provided anti-aircraft protection for the nation's capital on this property.[1]

Lingering geopolitical issues between the United States and the Soviet Union following World War II, fueled growing antipathy, resulting in a military arms race between the two nations.[2] The United States considered the expansion of Soviet communism in the world as a serious threat, and with the devastating 1941 Pearl Harbor attack only a decade removed, the possibility of enemy bombings with nuclear weapons was a genuine concern to the nation's leaders.[3]

In response, the U.S. Army and Army National Guard emplaced anti-aircraft weapons under the aerial approaches to major metropolitan areas in the continental United States, including Hybla Valley and in several other sites near the nation's capital.[4]

Hybla Valley was first the site of four 90 mm guns, an associated radar antenna, six barracks, and a mess hall for the 134 soldiers who operated and maintained the weapons and facilities.[5] The site featured a large circular, flat concrete pad with the guns placed equidistantly around the perimeter.[6] The 90 mm guns (designated because of the diameter of their barrels), weighed 19,000 pounds and were capable of reaching an enemy target at an altitude of 33,800 feet. The Army eventually replaced them with four 120 mm guns, which weighed 61,500 pounds and could reach a target at an altitude of 48,000 feet.[7] Thankfully, for the local community and the nation, those guns were allowed to remain silent.

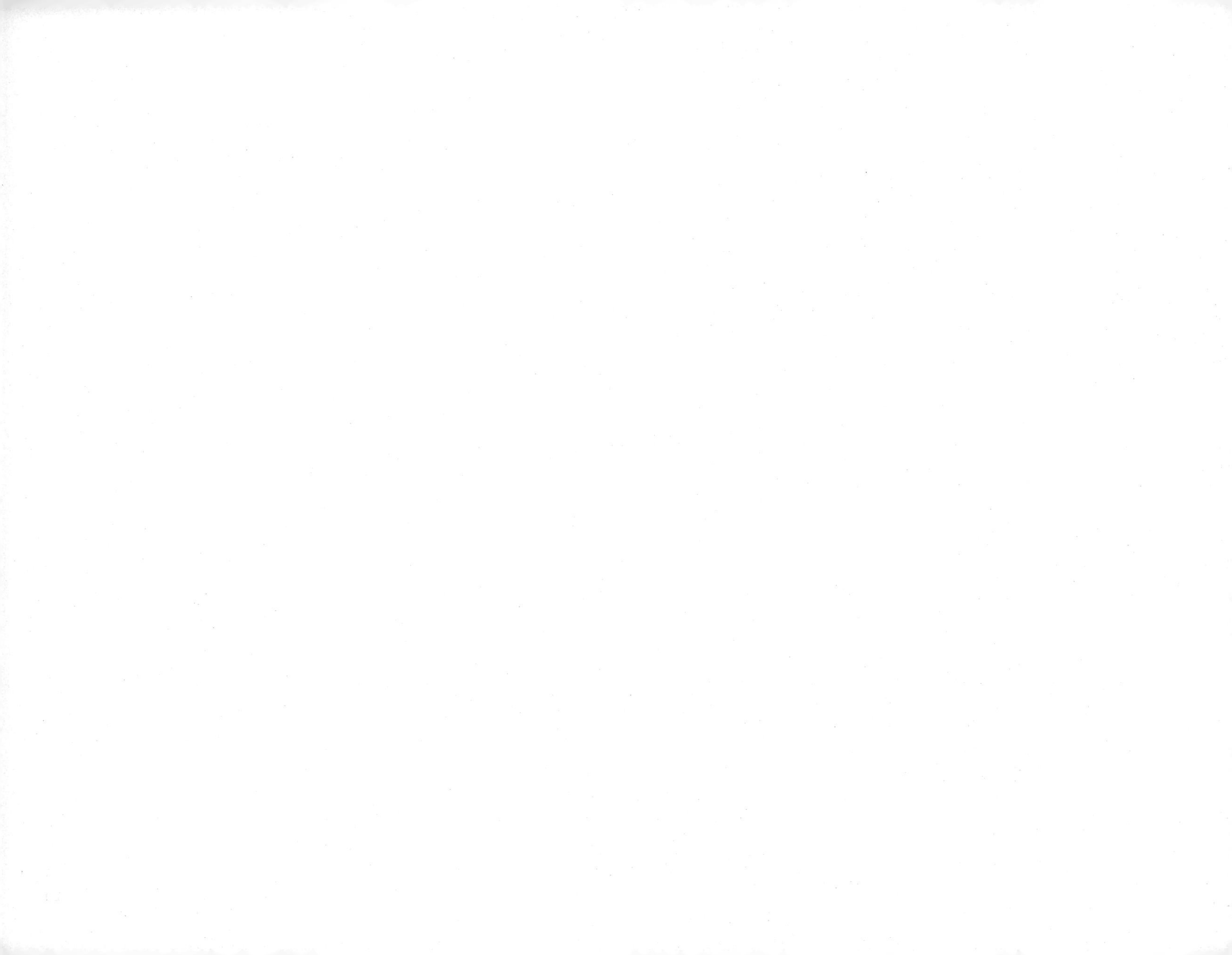

Chapter 7. The Age of Space Satellites —
The Naval Research Laboratory (1957-1971)

From 1957 to 1971, the United States Naval Research Laboratory (NRL) operated a classified radio communications system in Hybla Valley.[1] In the post-World War II world, advancements in technology progressed rapidly, and consequently, so did a proliferation of international satellites. U.S. military and civilian leaders committed themselves to developing precise monitoring systems to detect, track, and classify satellites, as well as foreign aircraft and submarines.[2] As part of that goal, the Naval Research Laboratory, in 1957, strategically chose Hybla Valley as the site to install one of its tracking stations.[3]

Since the early twentieth century, the U.S. Navy has been a leader advancing radio communication science, both domestically and internationally.[4] Hybla Valley's protective woods surrounded a large tract of open space that was ideal for the classified radar system, and central to its expanded monitoring initiative. The radar array consisted of a 434-foot diameter ring of 40 equally spaced antenna elements.[5]

Weeks before the October 1957 launch of Sputnik I, the former Soviet Union's first successful satellite, the NRL completed the Hybla Valley radar array.[6] The Soviet launch ushered in the modern space age and had a profound effect, sending shockwaves through the international community that had expected the United States to lead the world as the original pioneers in space.[7]

In an effort to catch up, NRL's scientific satellite Project Vanguard, which had been in development since 1955, was accelerated to "crash" (rapid acceleration or development) program status.[8] Vanguard I, launched in 1958, was the first solar-powered orbiting satellite, providing information on the Earth's physical properties.[9]

Meantime, some anticipated or predicted challenges of tracking Sputnik from the Hybla Valley radar array were confirmed and helped the NRL then to make modifications improving the accuracy of the tracking station's capabilities.[10] By 1971, the station was phased out, and the land was declared surplus.[11]

Chapter 8. The Federal Legacy of Parks Program

After decades of official use by the federal government, the Hybla Valley property was returned to Fairfax County and its residents in 1975. A year earlier, in September 1974, President Gerald Ford announced that the Fairfax County Park Authority would acquire 1,260 acres of the former Naval Research Laboratory-Hybla Valley property from the federal government through the Federal Legacy of Parks program.[1] The Hybla Valley land was one of 21 federal properties donated to 14 states, comprising 2,500 acres of land at this particular time.[2]

The Legacy of Parks program, established under President Richard Nixon, was an environmental conservation program designed to establish public parks and recreational areas, especially in urban areas.[3] This program was a targeted initiative, complementing the broader Surplus Federal Property Program for Parks and Recreation (now called the Federal Land to Parks Program), that had been transferring surplus federal property to local communities for decades.[4]

The Surplus Property Program/Federal Lands to Parks Program began as part of the Federal Property and Administrative Services Act of 1949. Originally, this Act required recipients of surplus federal properties through this program to pay 50 percent of the fair market value and use the property for public parks and recreation for 20 years.[5]

In 1970, Congress amended the Land and Water Conservation Act of 1965 (P.L. 91-485) allowing surplus federal properties for parks and recreation to be transferred at no cost provided they were to be used in perpetuity for public parks and recreation.[6] This agreement sought to encourage state and local governments to provide more parks and recreation areas. After 1970, the federal government transferred almost all properties at no cost in exchange for use of the property in perpetuity for public parks and recreation.[7] Lee District Representative and Fairfax County Park Authority (FCPA) board member, Carl Sell, made the request that the FCPA seek acquisition of the Naval Research Laboratory's Hybla Valley tract through the Legacy of Parks program once the property was declared surplus. In 1973 the General Services Administration

(GSA) declared the Hybla Valley tract surplus property, and the county submitted park development plans as part of its Legacy of Parks program request.[8] Thanks to this program, Fairfax County received the Hybla Valley property worth $10 million at no cost.[9]

In February 1975, the Fairfax County Park Authority invited Fairfax County residents to name the new park.[10] Over 600 names were submitted, many by school children and local scouts. The range of names contributed was wide, including Whitetail Game Reserve, Reefersville Park, John Wayne Park, and the Love Park. The winning entry of Huntley Meadows was submitted by Fairfax County residents, Oscar Harlow and 12-year old Joe Fields. The dedication was celebrated two months later on April 26.[11]

The Bureau of Outdoor Recreation deeded the property on November 26, 1975, at no cost, exclusively for a public park or public recreation purposes in perpetuity.[12] The Heritage Conservation and Recreation Service (HCRS) assumed program oversight and monitoring in 1978 when the agency was created. The National Park Service assumed oversight in 1981 when the HCRS was dissolved, and the National Park Service continues to ensure the property remains open and protected for the public.[13]

Note: In 1772, the property called "Huntley" was referenced as a tract of land. *Huntley Meadows Park Preliminary Master Plan Report*. 1976, p 31.

Chapter 9. The Boardwalk Restoration (2011)

One of the popular features of Huntley Meadows is the one-half mile boardwalk that transports visitors into the center of thriving wetlands.[1] In 1994, the boardwalk received its first upgrade. Creosote-treated railroad ties supported the original wood planks, installed by the Young Adult Conservation Corps.[2] The boardwalk was a perpetual maintenance burden for park staff. Heavy rains or beaver-caused flooding dislodged sections, sending them floating across the wetlands. During these years with higher than average rainfall in the wetlands, staff frequently shimmed or adjusted the boardwalk higher and higher until whole sections were floating.[3]

In 1994, the boardwalk was reinforced with steel anchors, new safety railings, and a modified route. The boardwalk now can withstand unusually high-water levels and storms. Its larger size accommodates increased visitor capacity and was the first Americans with Disabilities Act (ADA) fully compliant boardwalk in Northern Virginia.[4]

After eighteen-years of use and exposure to the elements, the original wooden boardwalk planks had worn down. In 2008, Fairfax County voters approved a $600,000 park bond to rebuild the boardwalk with safe and long-lasting materials.[5] In 2011, The TMG Construction Corporation of Purcellville, Virginia, led the restoration.[6] The boardwalk and the two observation platforms received new surface boards consisting of 100 percent high density polyethylene. The company created the non-slip replacement boards from 960,000 recycled milk jugs weighing 132,000 pounds and manufactured in Chicago, Illinois.[7] They replaced the creosote-treated wood that can be toxic to humans, animals, and insects, with a polyethylene-composite material, the most environmentally friendly, nontoxic plastic product on the market at the time.[8] This material has become recognized as a standard nationwide in parks and wildlife refuges.[9]

The two-month project was completed in three phases, ensuring that some of the board-walk remained accessible to visitors. The TMG team completed the restoration work on time and on budget even as they faced blistering August temperatures and September downpours. The Huntley Meadows Boardwalk Restoration project earned the TMG corporation the construction industry's Harry H. Mellon 2011 Award of Excellence for the Mid-Atlantic region, the Job Order Contracting (JOC) industry's highest honor.[10]

Chapter 10. The Wetlands Restoration (2013-2014)

Huntley Meadows is healthy, and its outlook as a haven for wildlife and vegetation is most promising.[1] Thanks to a major 2013 restoration project, the wetlands are larger, deeper, and are home to a wider diversity of life. Park staff regularly monitor plant and animal life, and control water levels to ensure a healthy ecosystem as weather and seasons change.[2]

But there were obstacles in getting the park to this point. Over decades, runoff from nearby housing developments and occasional droughts began to negatively alter the health and appearance of the Huntley Meadows wetlands.[3] What had once been a heathy hemi-marsh, home to a beautiful array of birds, had dried up into a muddy and silt-filled basin."[4]

According to the Fairfax County Park Service, in the 1980s three events combined to slowly reduce the wetlands' habitat and wildlife diversity:
- deposits of silt and debris;
- colonization and spread of invasive plant species;
- and constantly changing beaver activity.[5]

Beavers are recognized for their well-developed dam-building skills, and in Huntley Meadows these small engineers became all-too effective. Their damming created the life-giving hemi-marsh during the 1970s.[6] Eventually, the numerous dams reduced the marsh water levels in many pools and open spaces, impacting nesting and breeding birds, as well as critical vegetation. The decreasing water levels no longer supported the birds, driving them out. Invasive herbaceous species like cattail gained primacy, creating monotypic stands, and choking off other plant species.[7]

While some local stakeholders believed it was prudent to allow the wetlands to self-restore even if it required decades, others wanted to intervene and restore it as soon as possible for the enjoyment of visitors.[8] The goal of this effort would be to restore the hemi-marsh conditions of approximately 50 percent open water and 50 percent vegetation that provide an ideal environment to support a wide variety of wildlife. In 1991, Fairfax County approved $3 million for the wetland's restoration.[9]

The work was delayed 22 years because multiple engineering firms hired by the county were unable to secure dam and spillway permits as part of their proposed water-control systems. Their original plans were considered likely to cause major disruptions to the fragile park land.[10]

Wetland Studies and Solutions (WSSI), Inc., a major natural and cultural resources consultant in the Mid-Atlantic region, led and completed the restoration effort. WSSI demonstrated that their permanent water control structure did not require a dam or emergency spillways. They were able to limit disruptions to the park and wetlands during construction.[11] WSSI's water control system was now manageable by park engineers and could restore and retain the park's hemi-marsh.[12]

The restoration work commenced in April 2013 and concluded in March 2014.[13] Numerous indicators confirmed the effectiveness of the restoration, including areas of open water that increased from approximately nine-to-eighteen acres. Additionally, the restoration reduced the invasive cattail area from seven to one and one-half acres.[14]

WSSI's Huntley Meadows restoration project received numerous recognitions: A National Honor Award in the 2014 Engineering Excellence Awards competition by the American Council of Engineering Companies (ACEC), the 2013 Fairfax County Tree Preservation Award, and the 2013 Fairfax County Land Conservation Award.[15] The Huntley Meadows restoration project was recognized as a Gold Medal winner as part of the Virginia Governor's 2017 Environmental Excellence Awards.[16]

On May 10, 2014, members of the Fairfax County community gathered at Huntley Meadows to celebrate its reopening following the restoration work.[17]

Chapter 11. The Value of Our Wetlands

Huntley Meadows park contains freshwater wetlands, areas saturated with water for at least part of the year. Wetlands are recognized as one of the world's most important ecosystems.[1] These wetlands store and filter water and are an inexhaustible repository of food supporting many living groups.[2]

Wetlands are also home to countless species, from microbes to mammals. Additionally, they store carbon in their plants and soils instead of releasing it into the atmosphere as carbon dioxide.[3] Huntley Meadows is home to one of the few wetlands in Northern Virginia, and due to its location in a low valley, its wetlands collect silt, debris, and sewage that flow in from the surrounding community.[4,5] This invaluable filtering of pollutants improves local water quality, and is why wetlands are often referred to as our Earth's kidneys.[6]

Huntley Meadows' wetlands also provide flood control by catching and storing water in its basin.[7] Unfortunately, pristine wetlands like Huntley Meadows are becoming less common. More than half of our nation's wetlands have been lost since the eighteenth century.[8] Urbanization, climate change, and lack of understanding of how valuable these lands continue to be, are factors in wetland habitat loss.[9]

Chapter 12. The Value of Our Forests

The forests that encompass Huntley Meadows are critically important to the health of the community. Over half of the Commonwealth of Virginia is forested, but conversion to other uses such as residential and commercial development, well known to residents of Fairfax County, are steadily cutting into its acreage.[1] Additionally, trees have to adapt to a changing climate.[2]

The work of our trees is remarkable. Consider that 100 trees remove 53 tons of carbon dioxide and 430 pounds of other air pollutants per year. One-hundred mature trees catch about 139,000 gallons of rainwater annually.[3] One large tree can provide a day's supply of oxygen for up to four people, and serve as an invaluable habitat for wildlife, particularly birds.[4,5] Urban forests in areas like the Washington, D.C. metro region benefit the community by absorbing and slowing the precipitation before it reaches the ground.[6] They also provide watershed protection and prevent soil erosion.[7] Tall and dense trees also serve as a noise barrier in our communities.[8]

Healthy trees provide an ideal home for some of the most treasured and visible of animals, including more than 200 species of Huntley Meadows park birds.[9] Although endlessly desirable as subjects for photographers, birds can be fearsome predators. Few destructive, defoliating insects escape their pursuit. Importantly, bird-breeding seasons occur during insect population explosions. The plentiful young insects provide food for bird offspring and often spare our forests from insect destruction.[10]

Chapter 13. The Legacy of Norma Hoffman

"We need to recruit new generations of supporters to provide the eternal vigilance that is necessary to preserve and protect these fragile urban wetlands." ~ *Norma Hoffman*

The impact of Norma Hoffman on Huntley Meadows is deep. Without her leadership, a proposed four-lane highway would likely have caused immeasurable damage to the park.[1] Employing her unique skills and passion, Hoffman's vision of a permanently protected park for everyone's enjoyment caught fire with policymakers, stakeholders, and concerned citizens. Thankfully, she prevailed.

Born Norma Simon, she discovered her artistic gifts as a child. Her life's journey took her around the world, and her achievements include an impressive and lasting legacy. Among her most treasured accomplishments were the enduring bond of her family, her happy marriage of more than 70 years, and their daughter Lisa.[2]

"I was born and raised in Boston, Massachusetts," she recalled. "As early as three-years-old, I began to take dance lessons. I loved to dance. By the time I was a teenager, I was a paid chorus line dancer at the prestigious Latin Quarter Club. I did two shows a night, and was paid $40 a week, a very good sum at that time."[3]

For a young person, her job couldn't have been more exciting. The Latin Quarter Club, founded in Boston in 1937, was inspired by the Moulin Rouge, Paris, France's world-famous cabaret, theater, and music hall.[4] The club recruited the most beautiful dancers throughout the world, holding international tryouts, seeking that certain handful of young women like Hoffman, who they thought, sparkled and shined. The dancers received billing as "Latin Quarter Dancers of Today, Hollywood Stars of Tomorrow." Successful dancers were in impressive company, performing with some of the top entertainers of the day, including Jack Benny, Frank Sinatra, and Tony Bennett.[5]

And these were extraordinary times. Hoffman's native Boston was a dynamic city with a population of more than 770,000. Entertainment in the big band era provided an exciting escape from the distress of the twentieth century's great depression.[6,7] At the Latin Quarter Club, Hoffman appeared regularly with Milton Berle, one of the most popular comedians of the time, and other leading entertainers. At age 20, Hoffman was recruited by actress and singer Ethel Merman, to perform on Broadway in New York City.[8]

"I graduated from high school but didn't go on to college," said Hoffman. "My family couldn't afford to send me to college during the Depression. Then, I met and married my husband Fred Hoffman, and we moved to Washington, D.C. where he took a job as a newspaper reporter."[9] Fred Hoffman went to work for the Associated Press news service and later served as the Principal Deputy Assistant for the U.S. Secretary of Defense.[10]

Settling in Alexandria, Virginia, Hoffman began her local career in the offices of two members of congress. Following that, she worked for the Potomac Appalachian Trail Club, where she developed expertise and a love of environmental protection issues.[11] This experience began decades of distinguished volunteerism that earned her local, regional, and national recognition. When Hoffman applied to serve as a Huntley Meadows Park volunteer, she included the words "Let's talk" on her application.[12] Thus, she began a conversation lasting over decades, emphasizing the need to preserve this priceless land, and above all, teaching children about the importance of nature and the environment.[13]

Hoffman's lasting impact came into sharp relief in 1978 when she engaged her organization, the Citizens Alliance to Save Huntley Meadows Park (CASH,) after an approved four-lane highway threatened to cut through the three-year old park.[14] In June 1979, community leaders approved a bypass connecting Route 1 with Telegraph Road, via Lockheed Boulevard. Part of a larger Springfield bypass project, policymakers believed that the bypass could help stem the tide of ever-increasing traffic congestion in Southeastern Fairfax County.[15] The idea of a bypass was not new, however. In the late 1960s, Fairfax County began planning for the bypass, and included as part of the 1975 park master plan, a road to bisect the park on its northern edge.[16]

Additionally, state and local highway planners designed the larger regional route to cut through four additional parks, Pope's Head, Burke Lake, South Run, and Huntsman.[17] In July 1983, the National Park Service approved the expansion of the highway bypass through Huntley Meadows.[18] Fairfax County approved a bond issue valued at $135 million for 14 road construction projects, including the Lockheed Boulevard Connector.[19] In response, CASH enlisted scientific, legal, and grassroots community help. Gathering signatures opposing the highway and leading events such as a 1985 walk along the proposed route, Hoffman provided critical leadership. "We are adamant about taking the road out of the park," stated Hoffman. "We understand the need for a transportation route, considering the anticipated growth in the area, [but] we think there should be an alternate route."[20]

CASH, the Northern Virginia Conservation Council, and concerned citizens demanded an environmental study because of their concern about the increased air and noise pollution that the connector threatened to cause. An initial Fairfax County commissioned environmental-impact study did not reveal any potentially serious damage to the park. Unconvinced, Hoffman pressed the Department of the Interior to perform its own environmental study, and requested that they stop the road project based on a lack of information supporting it.[21]

In 1987, the Interior Department released a study confirming that permanent damage would be done to the park by the bypass road.[22] In December 1990, Fairfax County officials announced that they would abandon plans to build the connector after the Department of the Interior notified them that they would not permit the road. The Environmental Protection Agency, the Fish and Wildlife Service, and the National Marine Fisheries Service then recommended to the Army Corps of Engineers to reject the Fairfax County permit to build the road extension.[23]

Norma Hoffman co-founded the non-profit Friends of Huntley Meadows Park (FOHMP) in 1985. The organization has more than 400 members and is dedicated to preserving these rare and invaluable wetlands in Northern Virginia. FOHMP also provides year-round educational and volunteer opportunities and actively advocates for the protection of the wetlands.[24]

Hoffman, through her organization, Friends of Historic Huntley, led the effort to purchase and restore Historic Huntley, the nineteenth century home of Thomson Francis Mason.[26] Funding for the restoration came from approved local Fairfax County bonds, and a $100,000 Save America's Treasures grant secured by Virginia's 8th congressional district Representative James Moran.[25] Today the 1,400 square-foot home is a living museum that through public tours, lectures, and teas, teaches visitors about plantation life in the nineteenth century, the gentry, and farming.[27, 28]

Hoffman continued as a volunteer at Huntley Meadows Park for nearly four decades. She was honored with the Fairfax County Park Authority's highest volunteer service award, received the annual Distinguished Volunteer Service Award from the Virginia Recreation and Park Society, and in the week before her death in 2017, was named an Outstanding Volunteer by the National Association of County Park and Recreation Officials.[29]

In 1992, the Sierra Club named her one of its 100 Environmental Heroes.[30] For decades, Hoffman taught thousands of children about nature as well as the responsibility and rewards of being environmental stewards. A park authority board resolution noted that she tirelessly served community children in a 30-year crusade to imprint an appreciation for the environment through countless classes, hikes, and engaging stories.[31]

In 2013, the Visitor Center at Huntley Meadows Park was named in Hoffman's honor. In recognition of her leadership, she received more than 30 county, state, and national awards, including the Virginia Wildlife Federation's "Conservationist of The Year." [32]

Believing that we have the obligation to help the less fortunate, Hoffman volunteered time to her community in senior citizen centers, social service agencies, and tutored disadvantaged children. And it was with children that her heart belonged. Nothing gave her more pleasure than teaching children about Huntley Meadows and its beauty and importance. Her family established the Norma Hoffman Financial Assistance Program that provides scholarships and ensures that disadvantaged students have access to Huntley Meadows Park field trips, now and in the future.[33]

As a result of the leadership and advocacy of Norma Hoffman, Huntley Meadows belongs to all of us. We should, we must, and we will preserve and protect Huntley Meadows.

Chapter 14. Photographs

"It's only a little planet, but how beautiful it is." ~ Robinson Jeffers

"I believe the world is uncomprehensively beautiful — an endless prospect of magic and wonder." ~ Ansel Adams

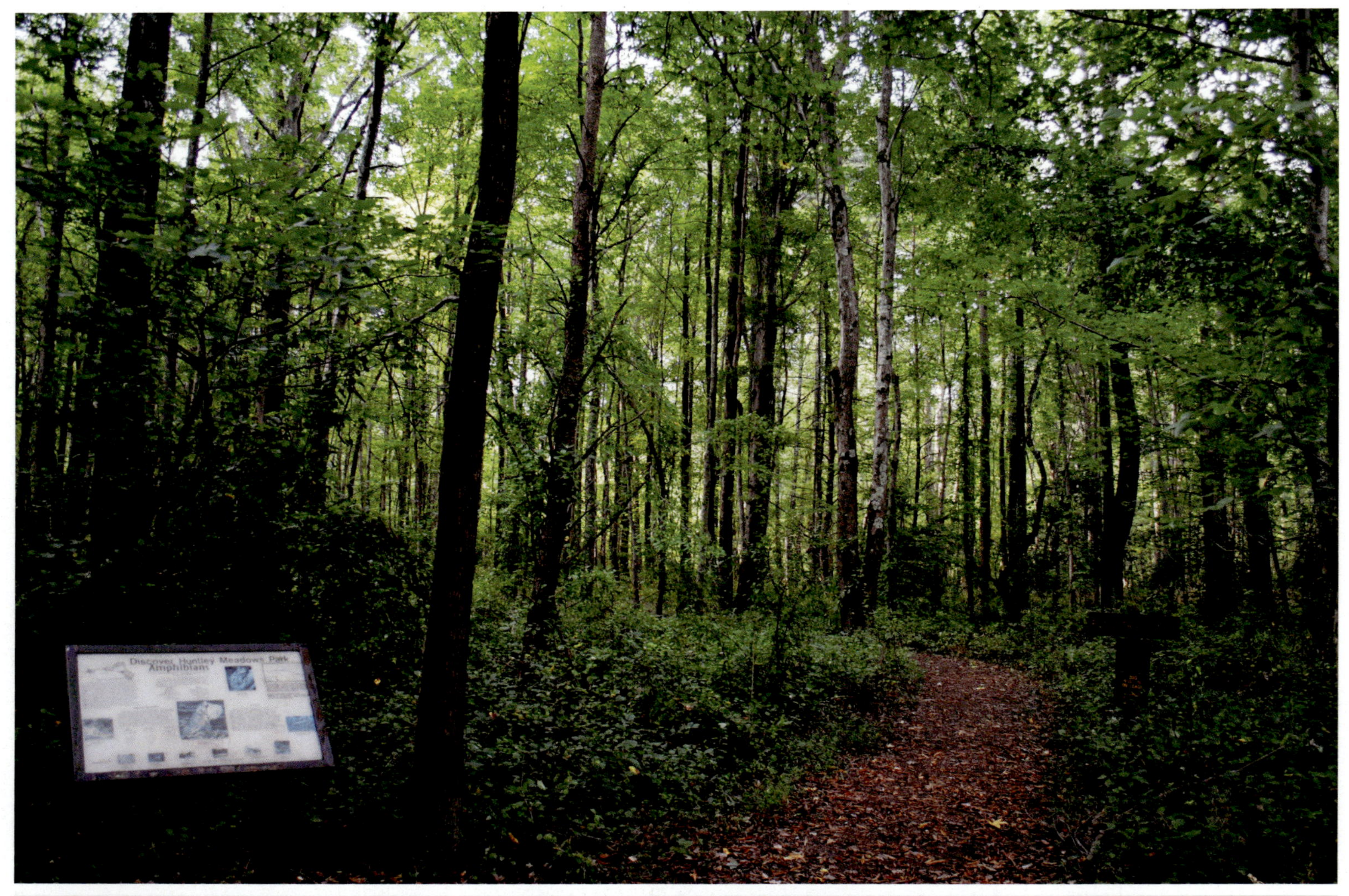

1. The Pond Trail, near the South Kings Highway entrance, is one of numerous trails enjoyed by both humans and their faithful canines.

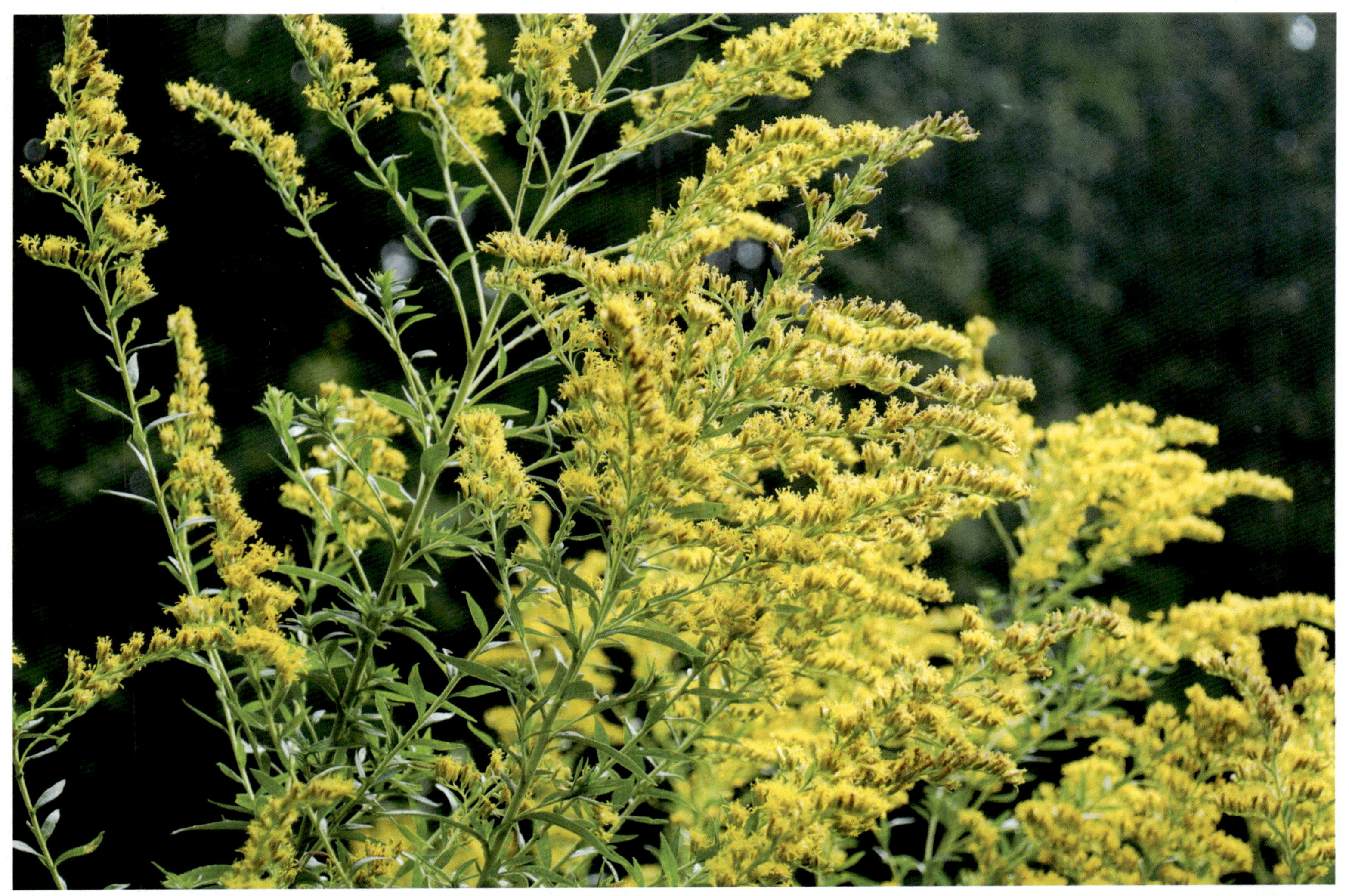

2. Goldenrod in the South Kings Highway Meadow are sun-loving plants and favorite pollinating stations for butterflies and bees.

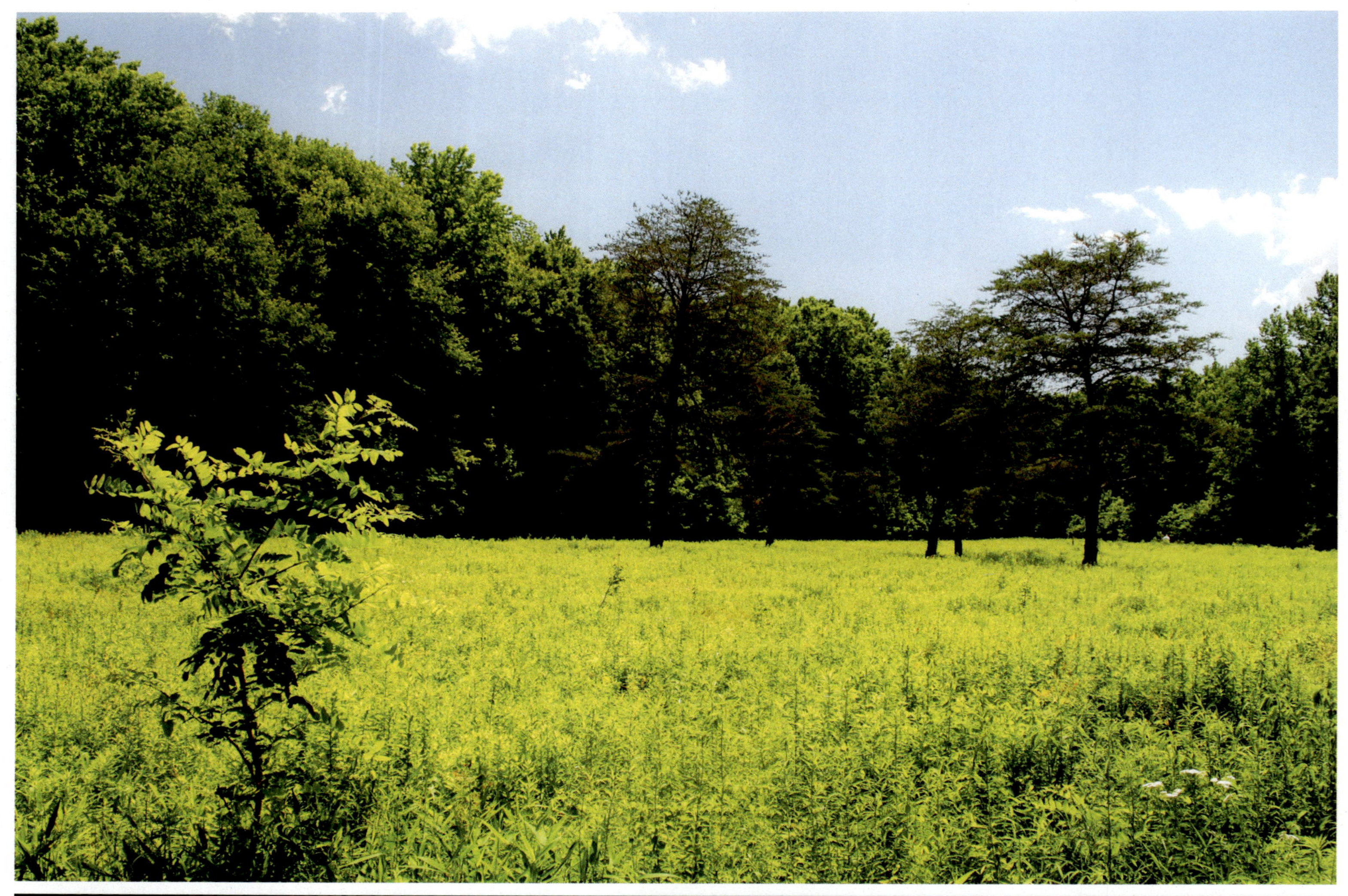

3. Spring arrives boldly in the South Kings Highway meadow. To see it like this, visit early in the season before wildness takes over.

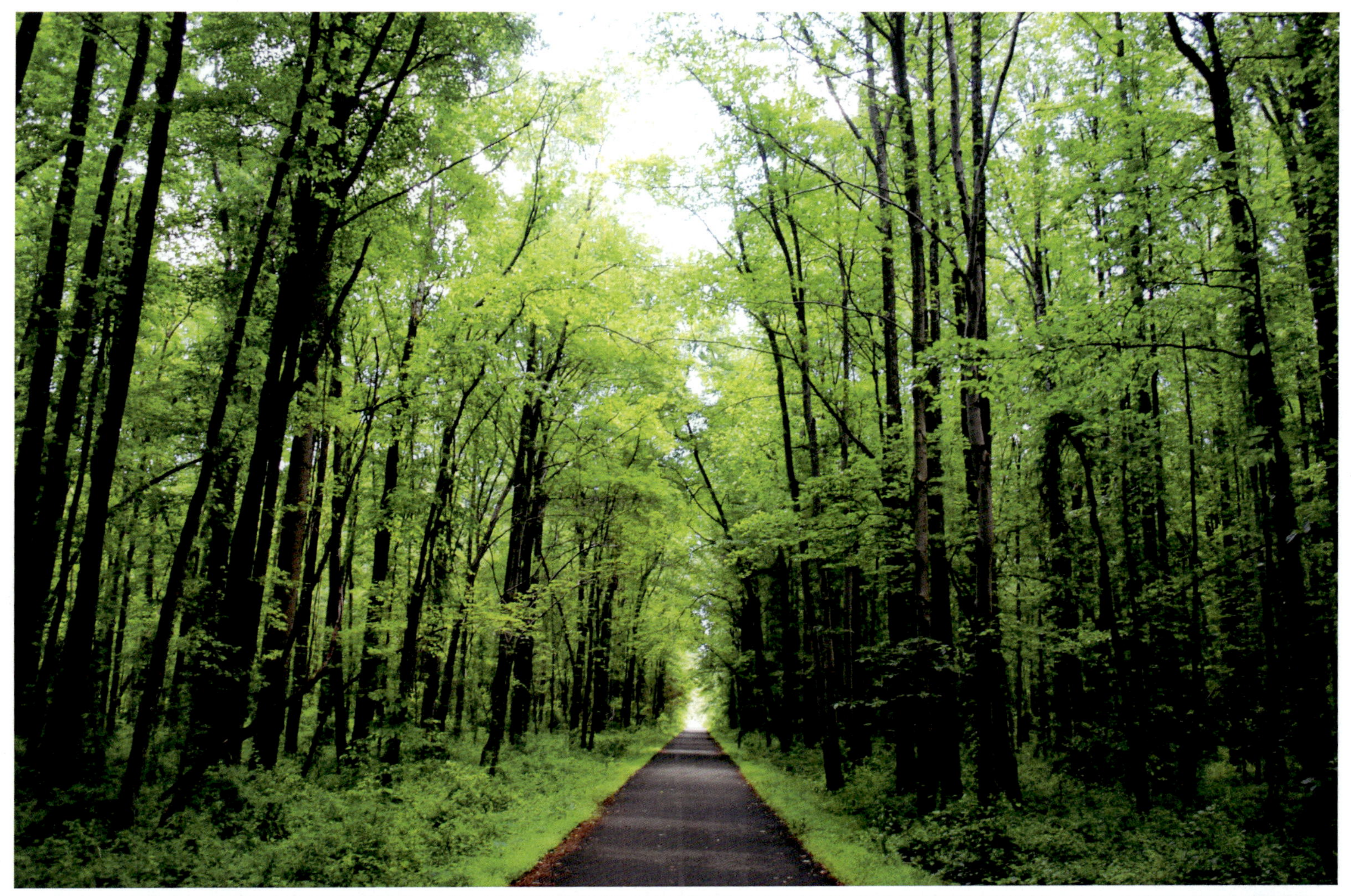

4. Springs' warmth and light animate forests on the path from the South Kings Highway entrance leading to the marsh overlook.

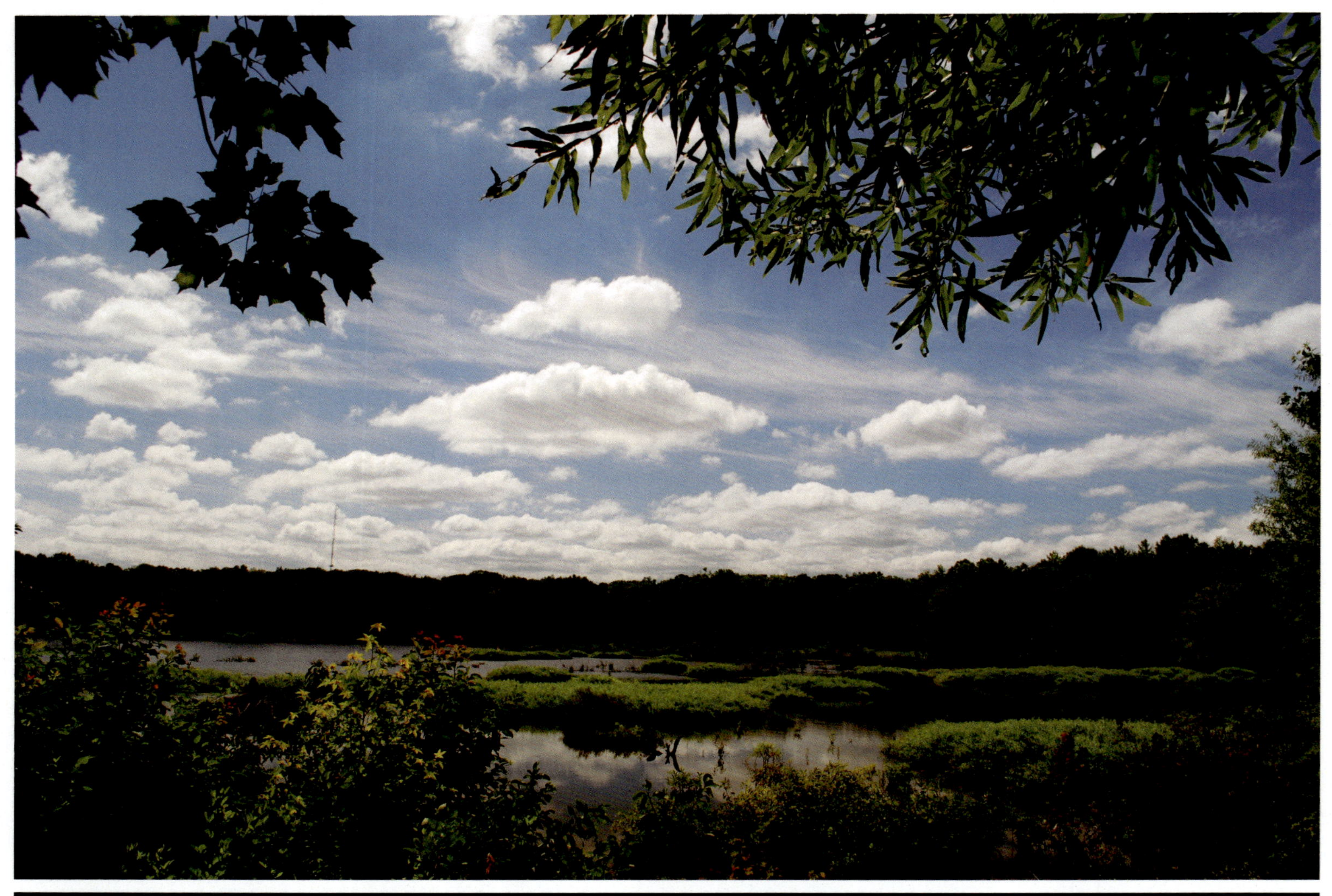

5. The observation deck on the South Kings Highway side of the park is a quiet spot for viewing nature.

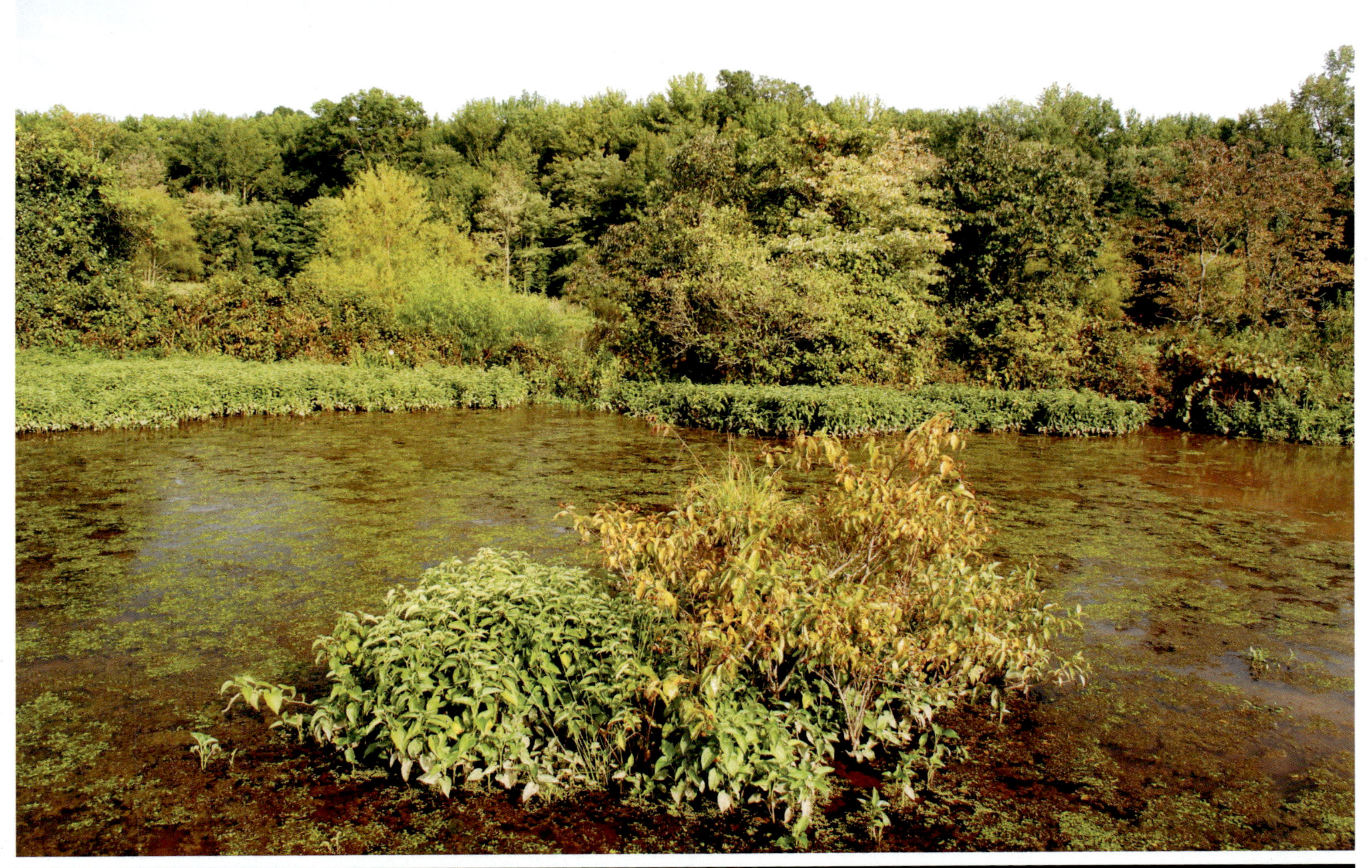

6. Forests and wetlands blend seamlessly. Here, diverse life constantly interacts with, renews, and regenerates the landscape.

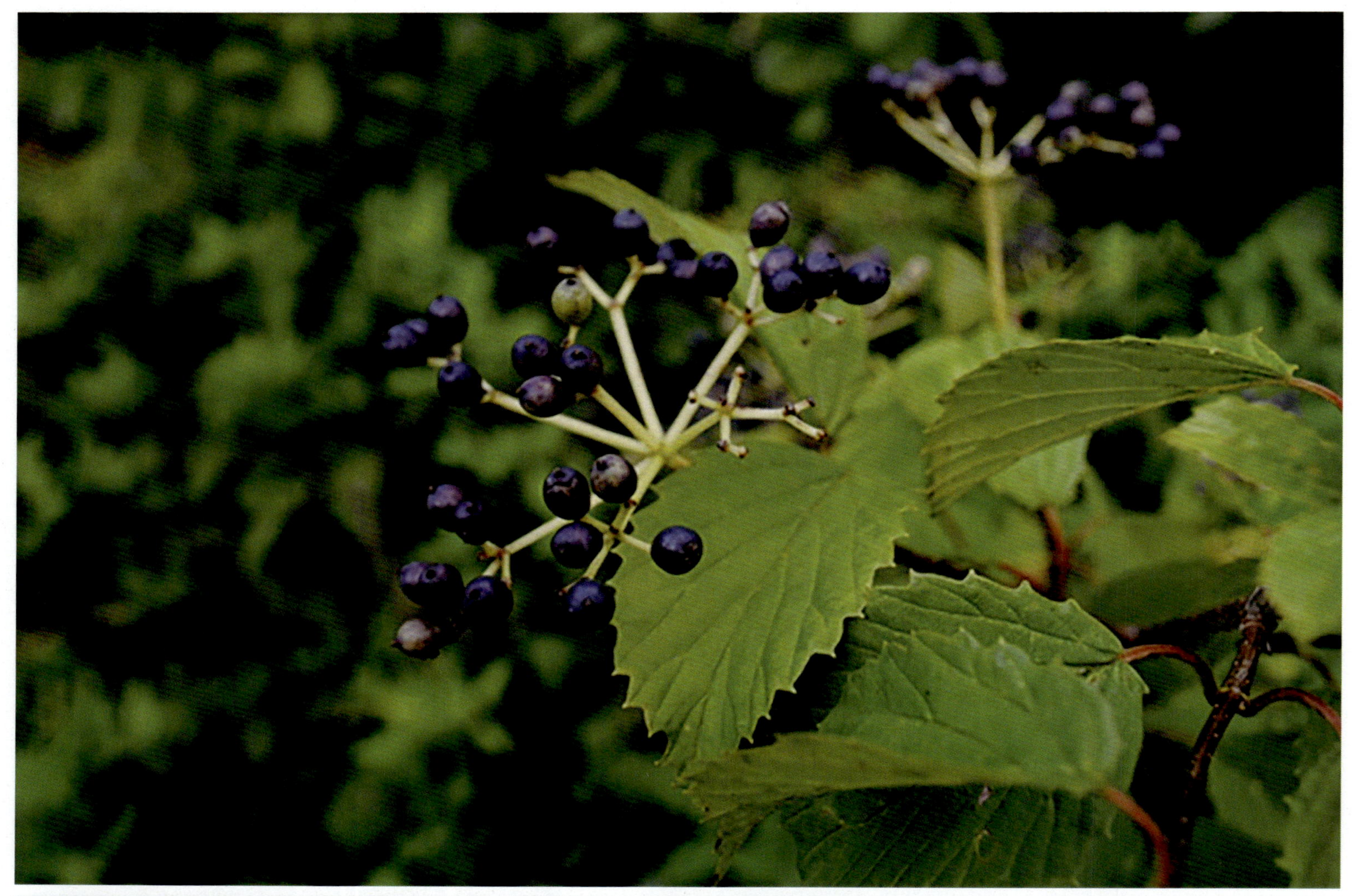

7. Viburnum dentatum (also known as southern-arrowwood) is a native shrub. Birds enjoy its dark blue berries, and the plant also has medicinal uses.

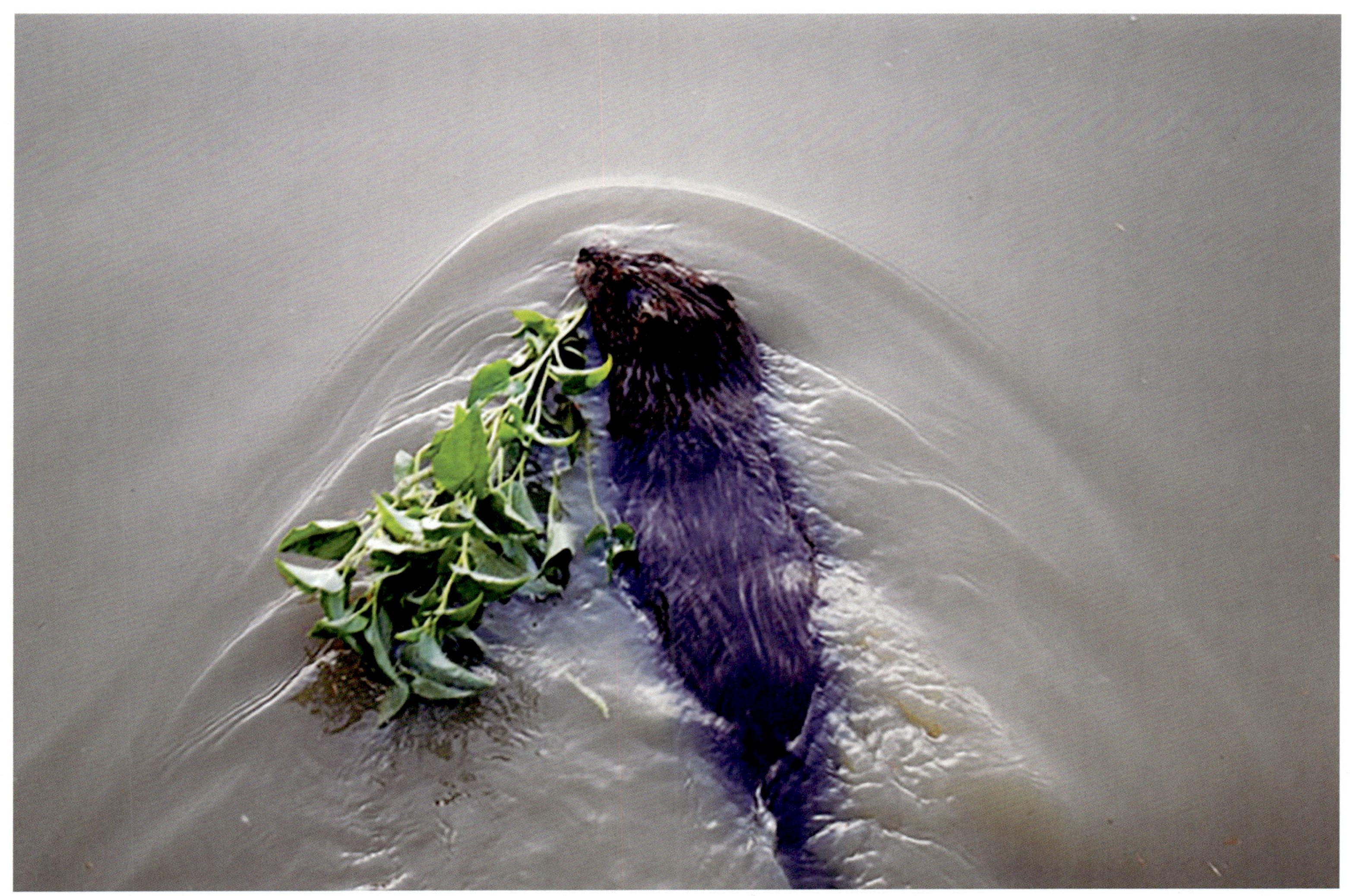

8. Beavers are small but mighty environmental engineers. They can weigh up-to 60 pounds and live more than 20 years. Beaver damming is responsible for creating the Huntley Meadows wetlands we enjoy.

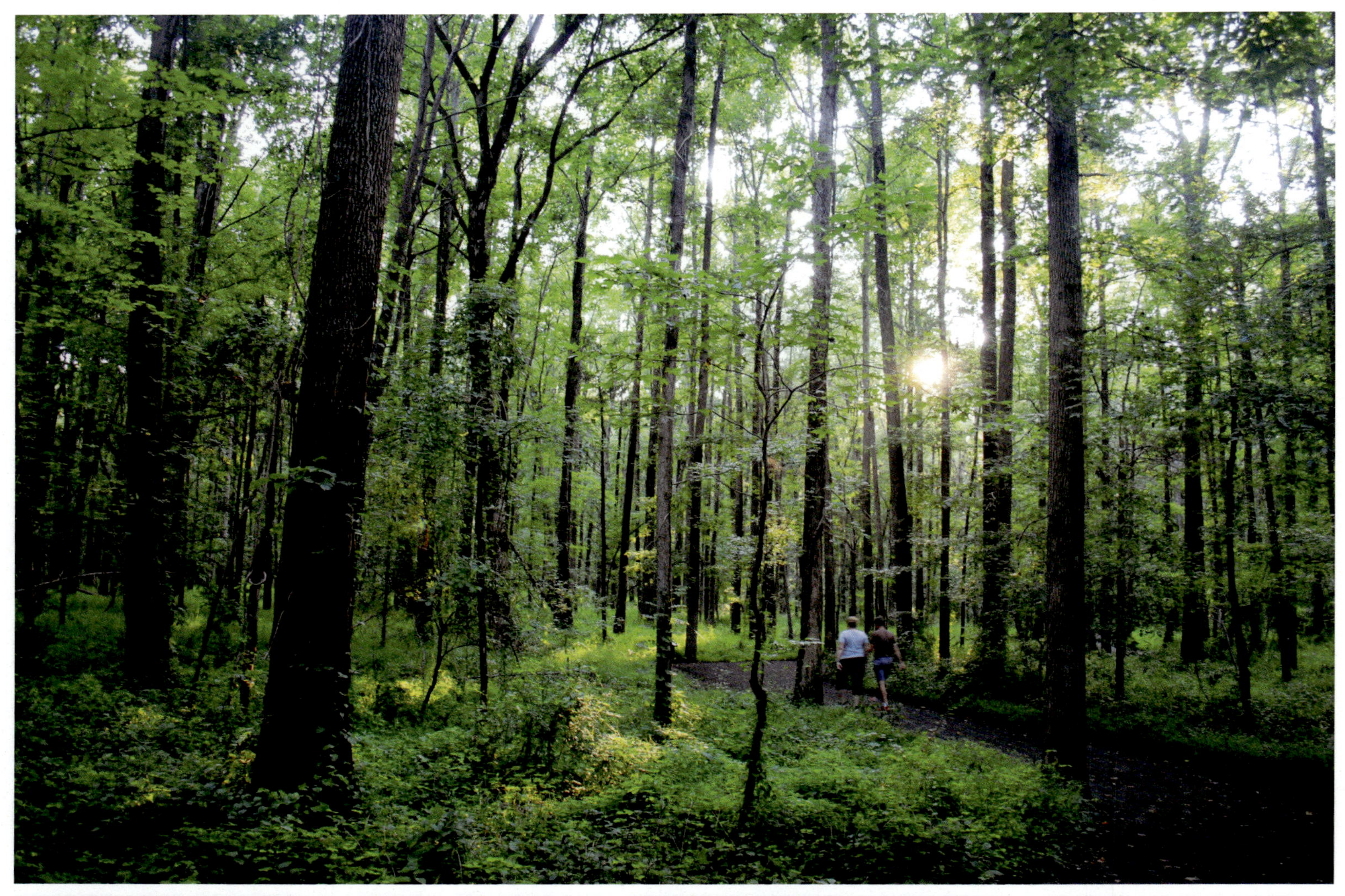

9. Late afternoon walks reward visitors with relief from summer heat as well as increased activity of wetland birds, beavers, and deer, among other animals.

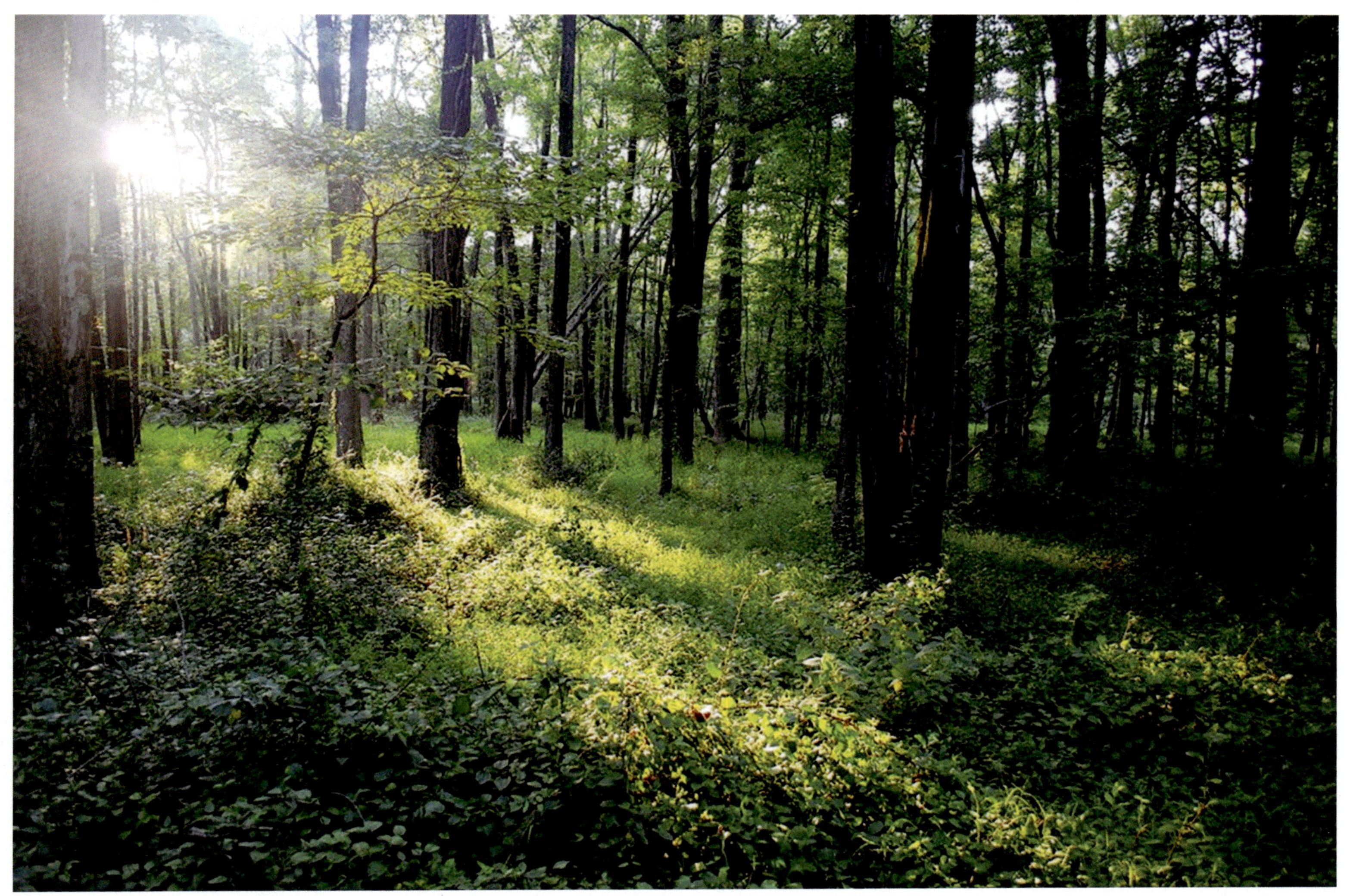

10. Streaming light cuts through the forest on a late summer afternoon.

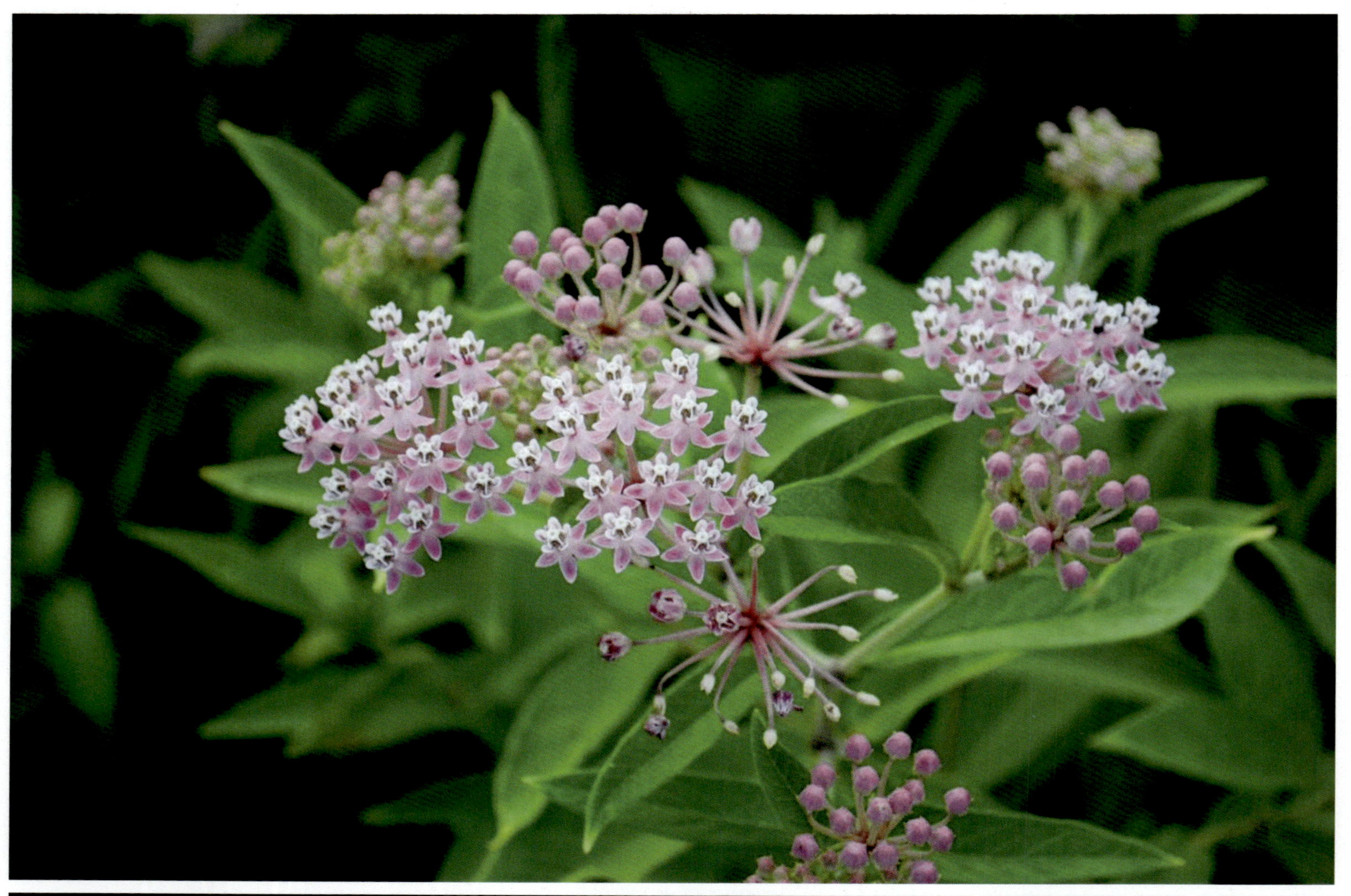

11. Milkweed is a perennial herb with medicinal uses. It is attractive to beetles, bees, and monarch butterflies that lay their eggs on its leaves.

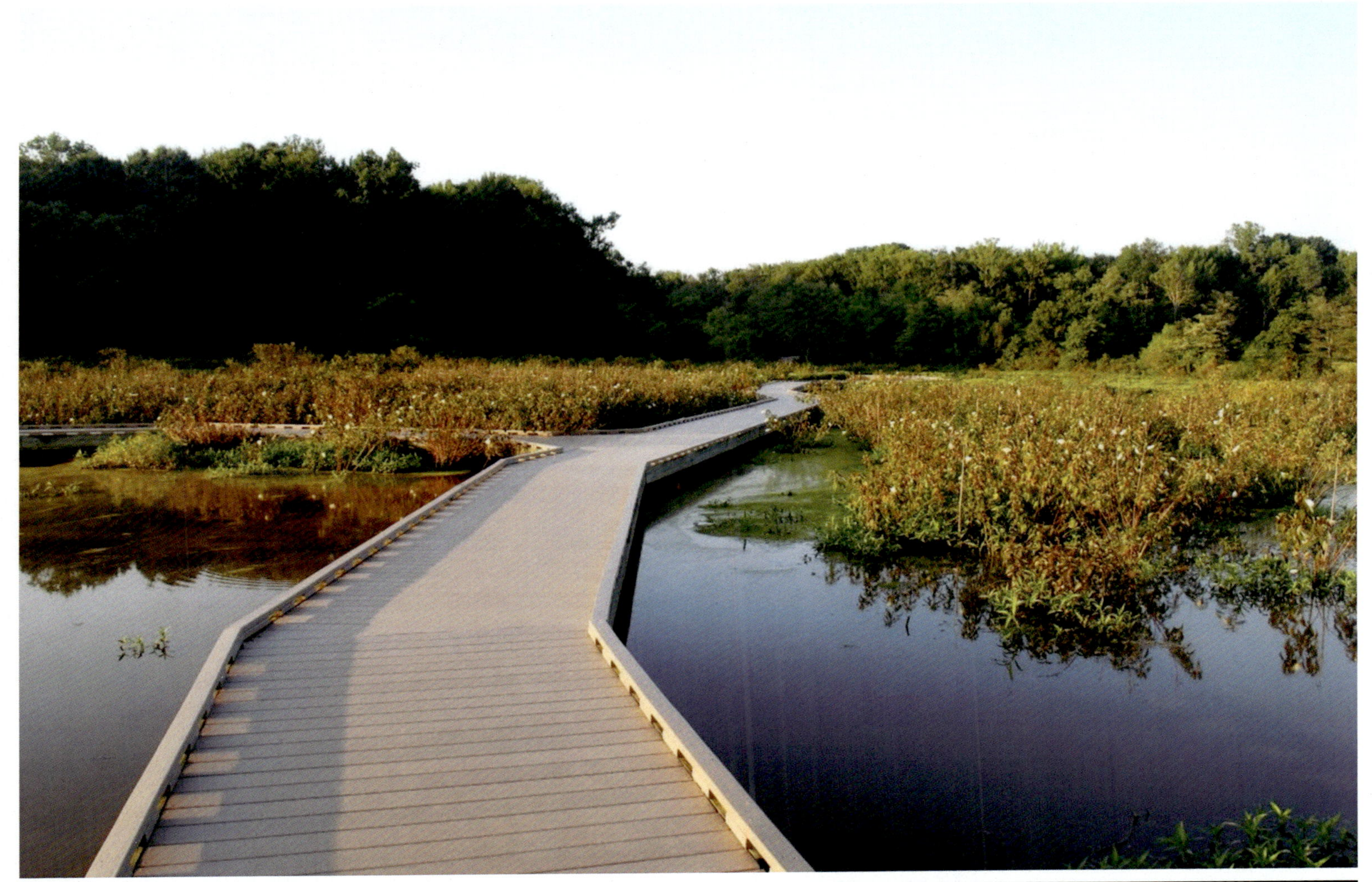

12. This durable boardwalk brings visitors from the periphery into the heart of nature.

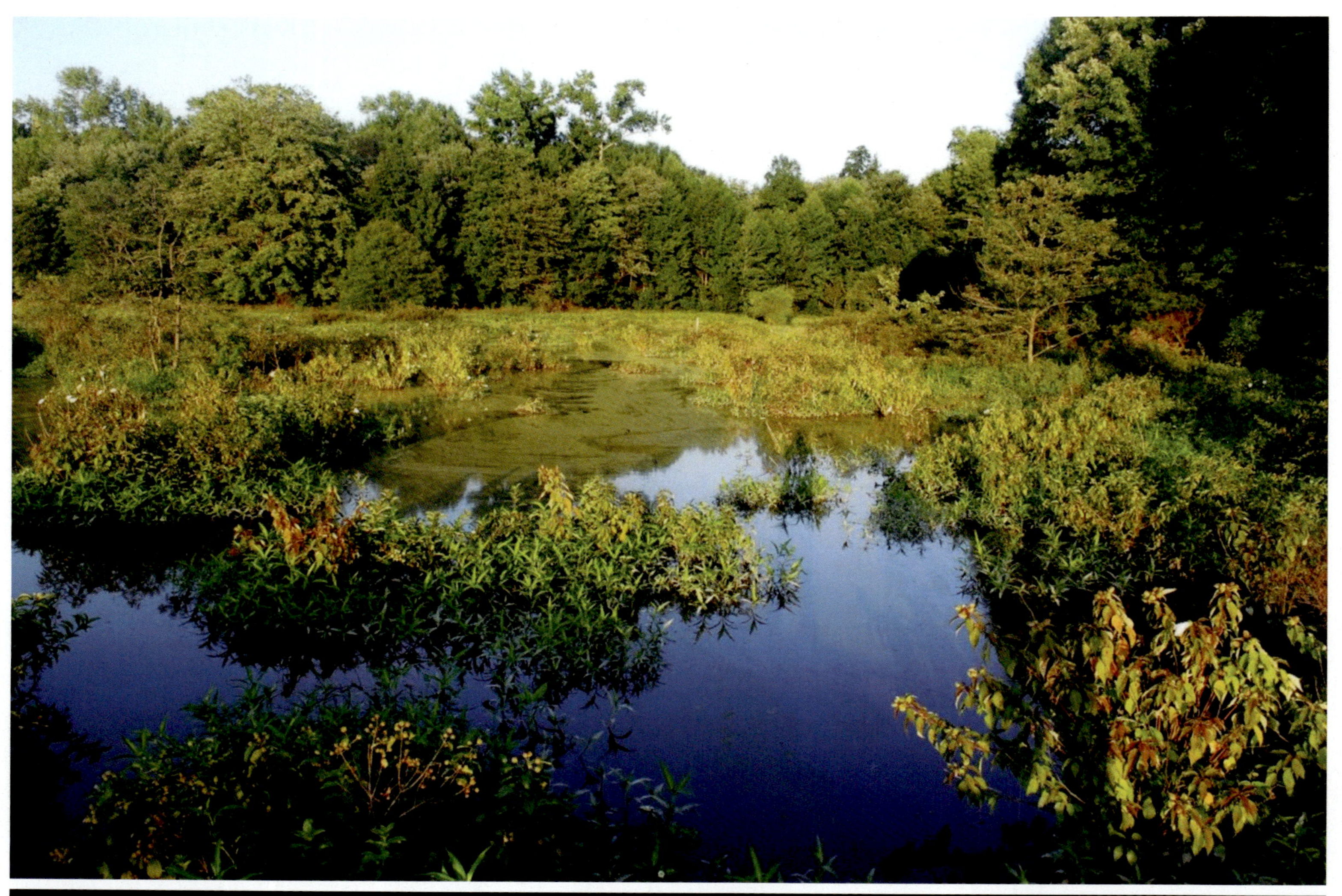

13. Summer evening serenity. This peaceful moment was punctuated with a cacophony of sound thanks to active frogs, birds, and insects.

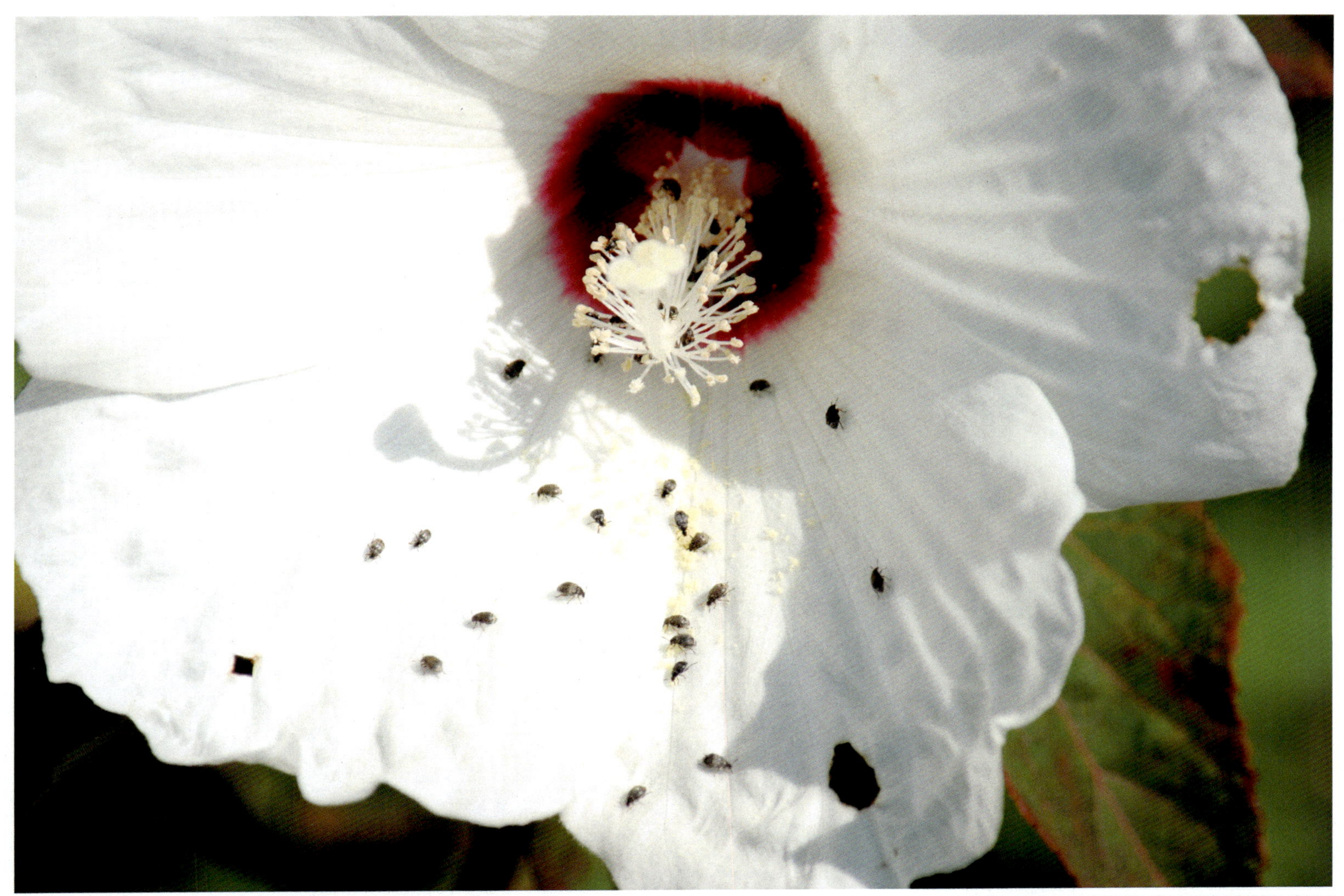

14. The swamp rose is a perennial shrub that can grow up to seven feet. Its blossoms are large, fragrant, and home to small insects.

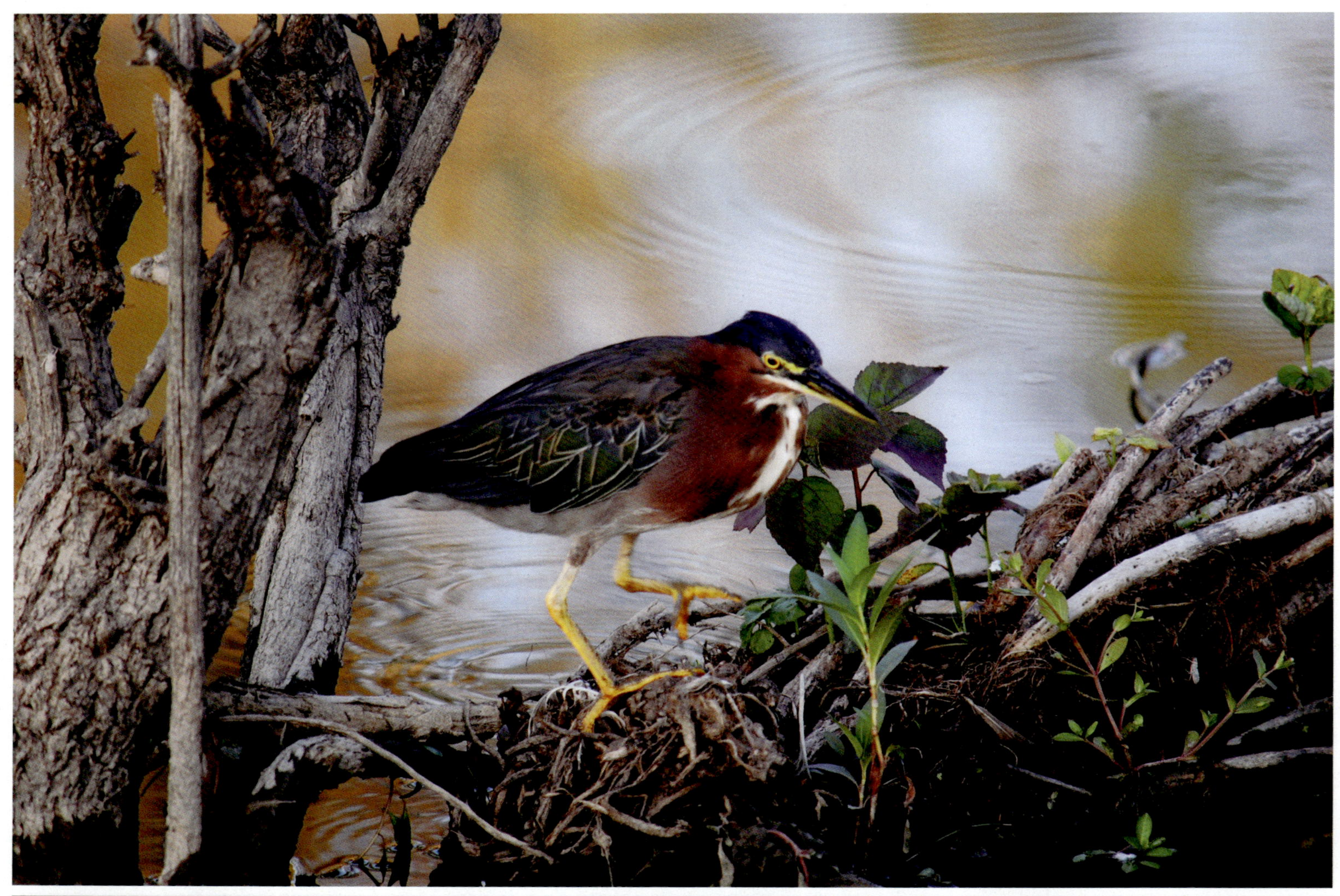

15. The green heron, shown here in summer, is one of the smallest in the heron family. These solitary birds create lures for prey from insects, feathers, and other small objects.

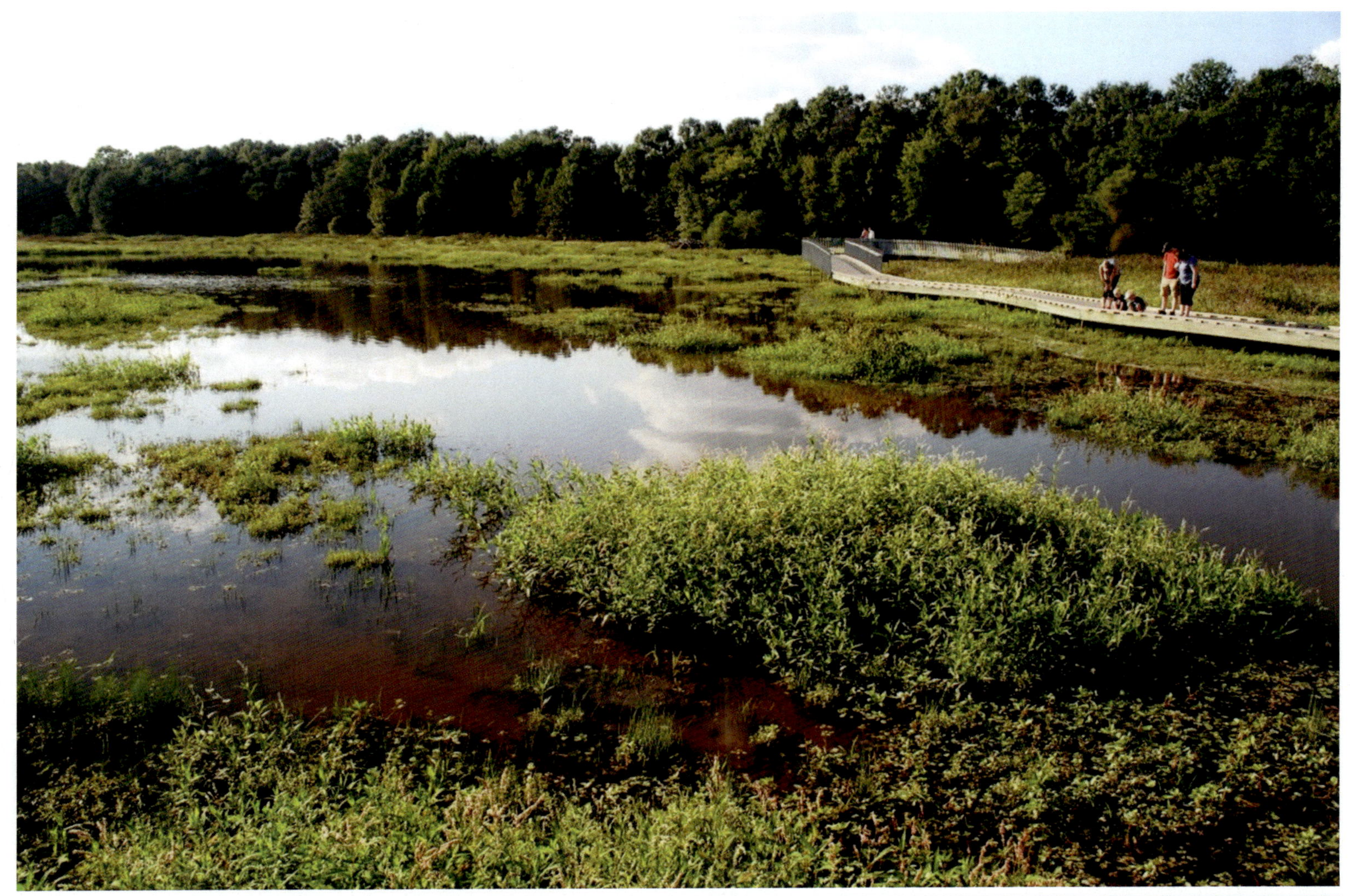

16. Each day at Huntley Meadows, something meaningful draws and fascinates visitors of all ages.

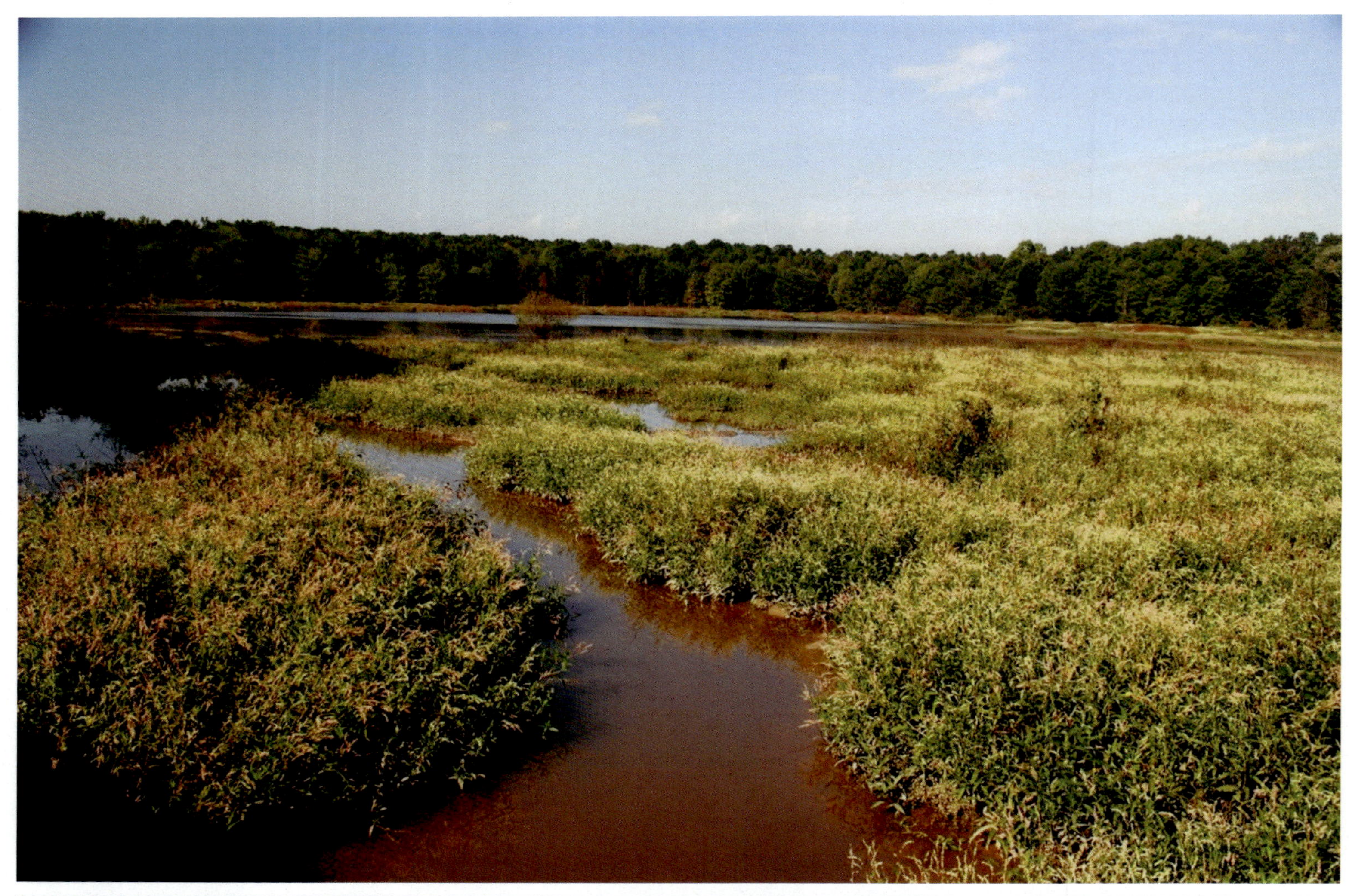

17. The central marsh in September boasts a healthy variety of herbaceous plants, especially after a record summer rainfall.

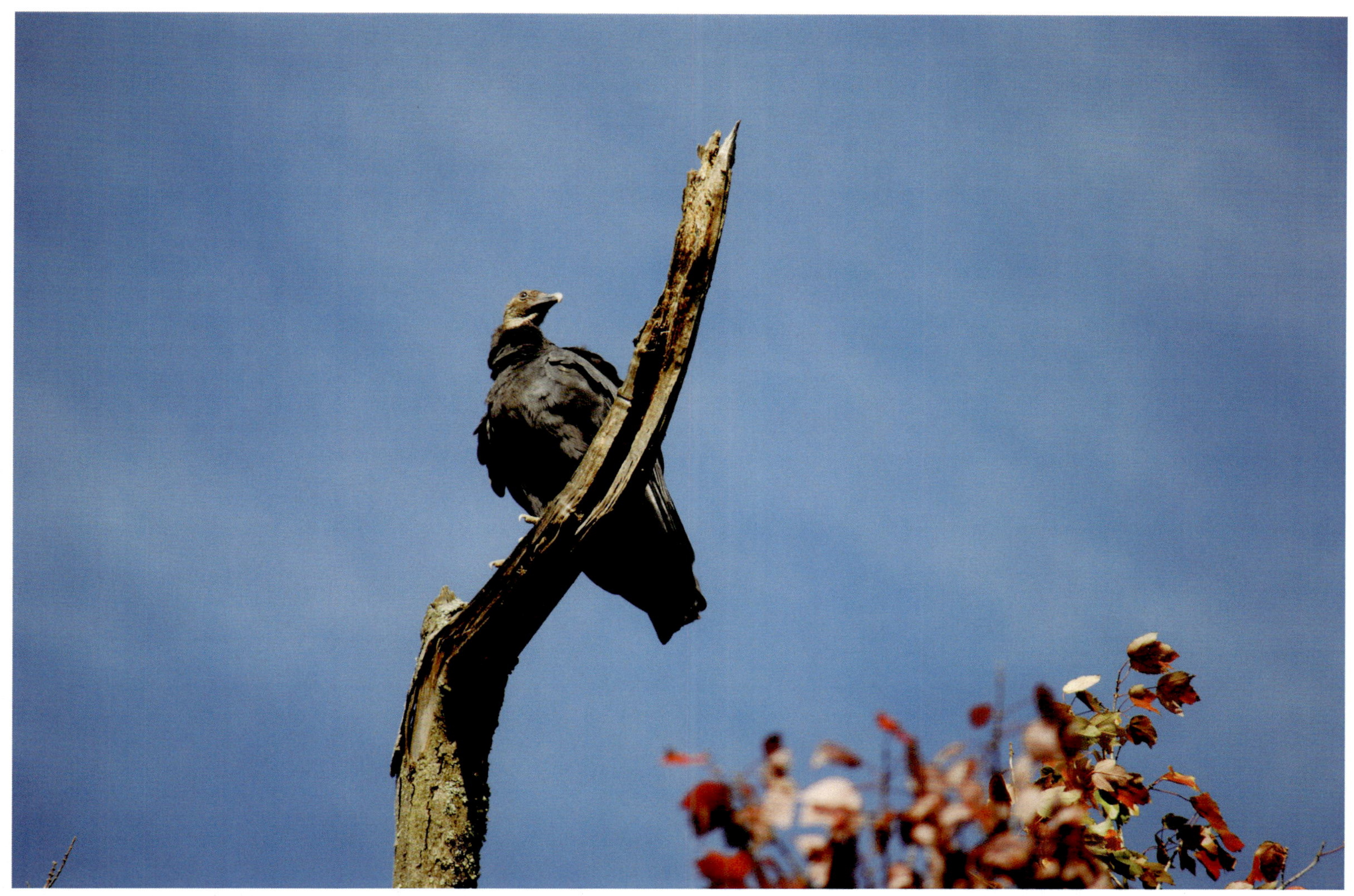

18. The black vulture is a federally protected migratory bird frequently seen in Huntley Meadows. These scavengers can have five-foot wingspans.

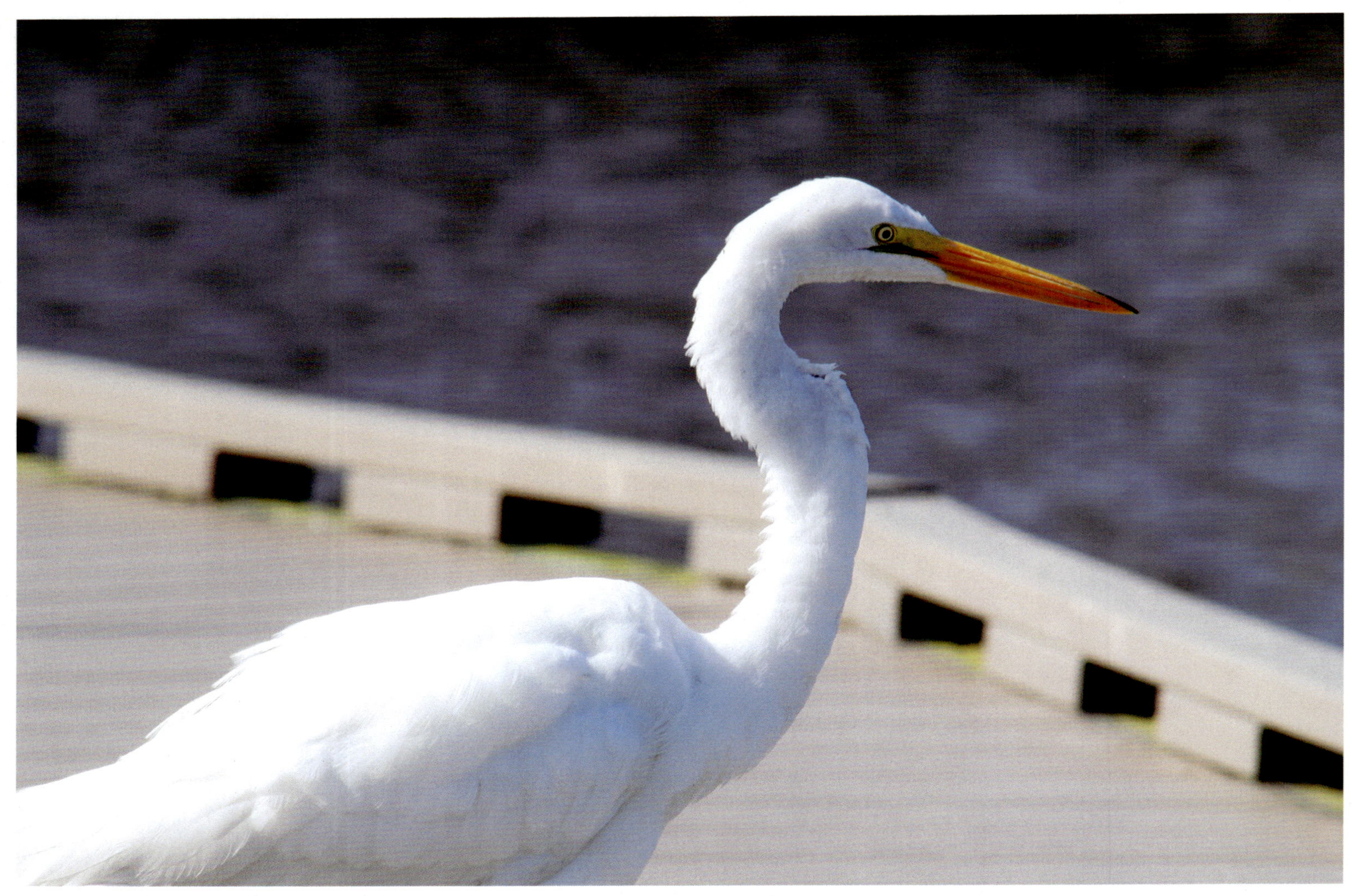

19. The great egret, a graceful and strikingly beautiful wading bird, was nearly driven to extinction in the 19th century. Thanks to conservation efforts, they thrive on every continent.

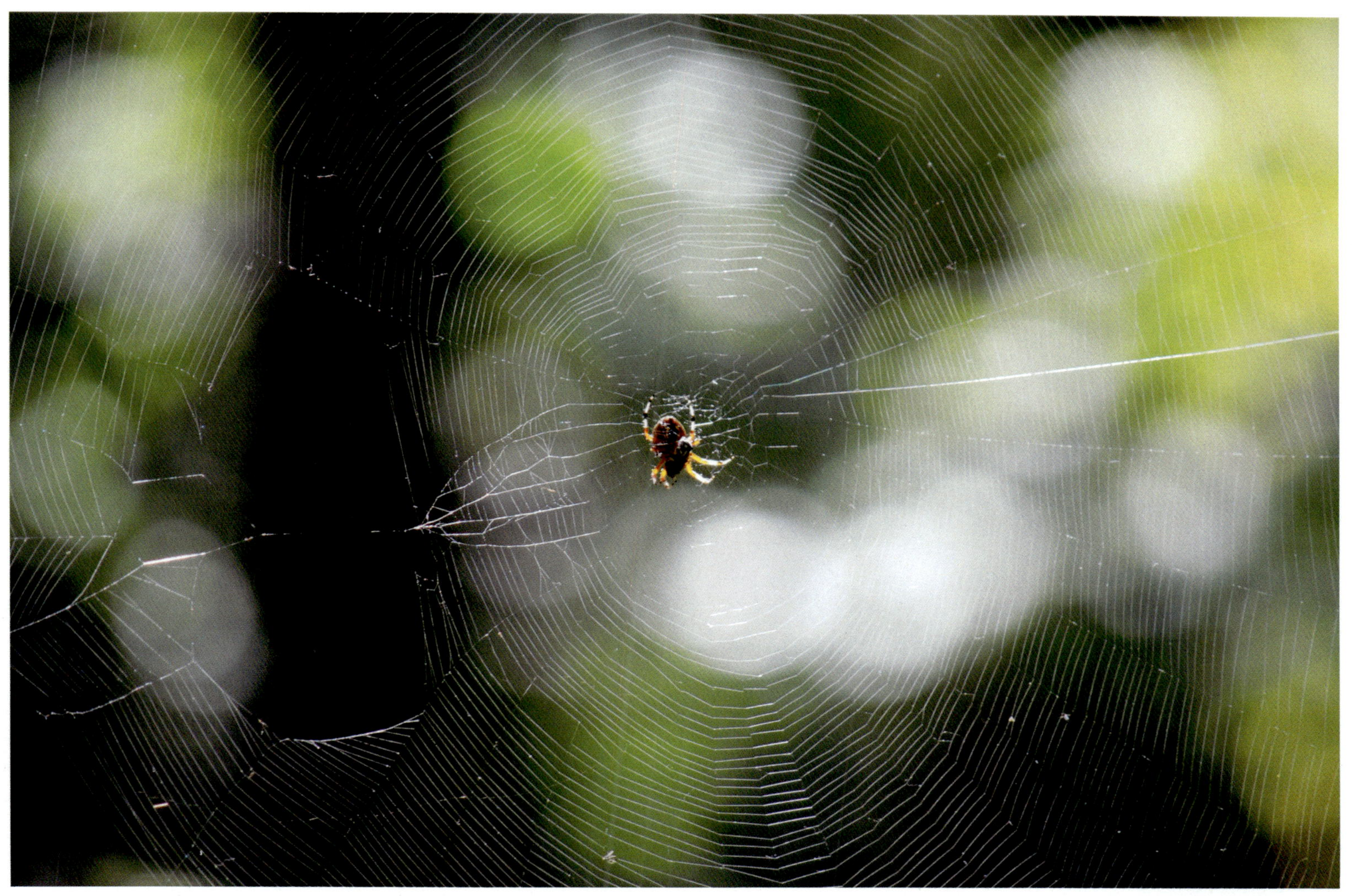

20. The orb weaver spider constructing a web, creates one of the world's most remarkable engineering feats. Their webs serve as both a home and as a trap for food.

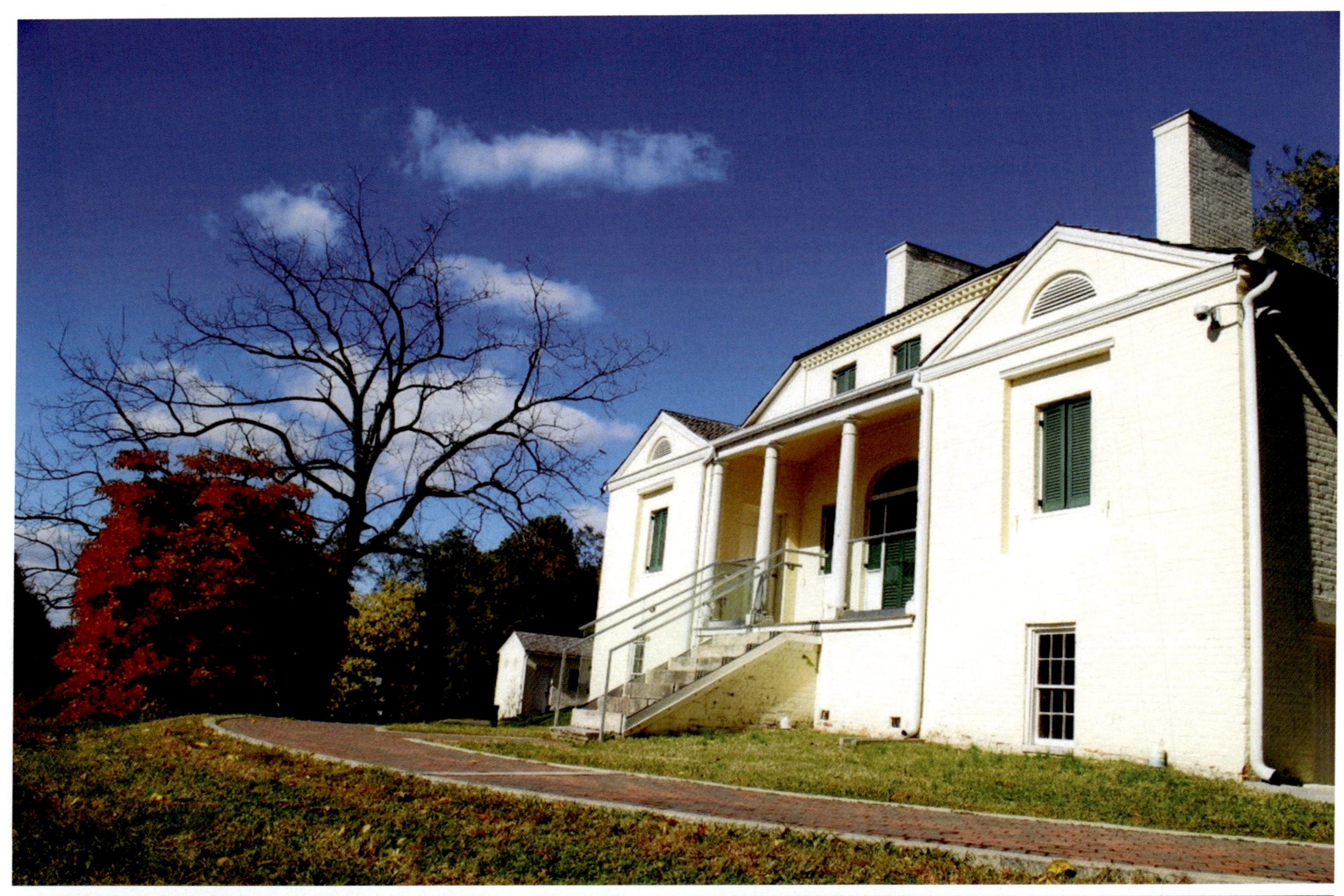

21. Overlooking Huntley Meadows Park is the historic Huntley house. Built in the early nineteenth century, it served as a summer retreat for the descendents of George Mason IV.

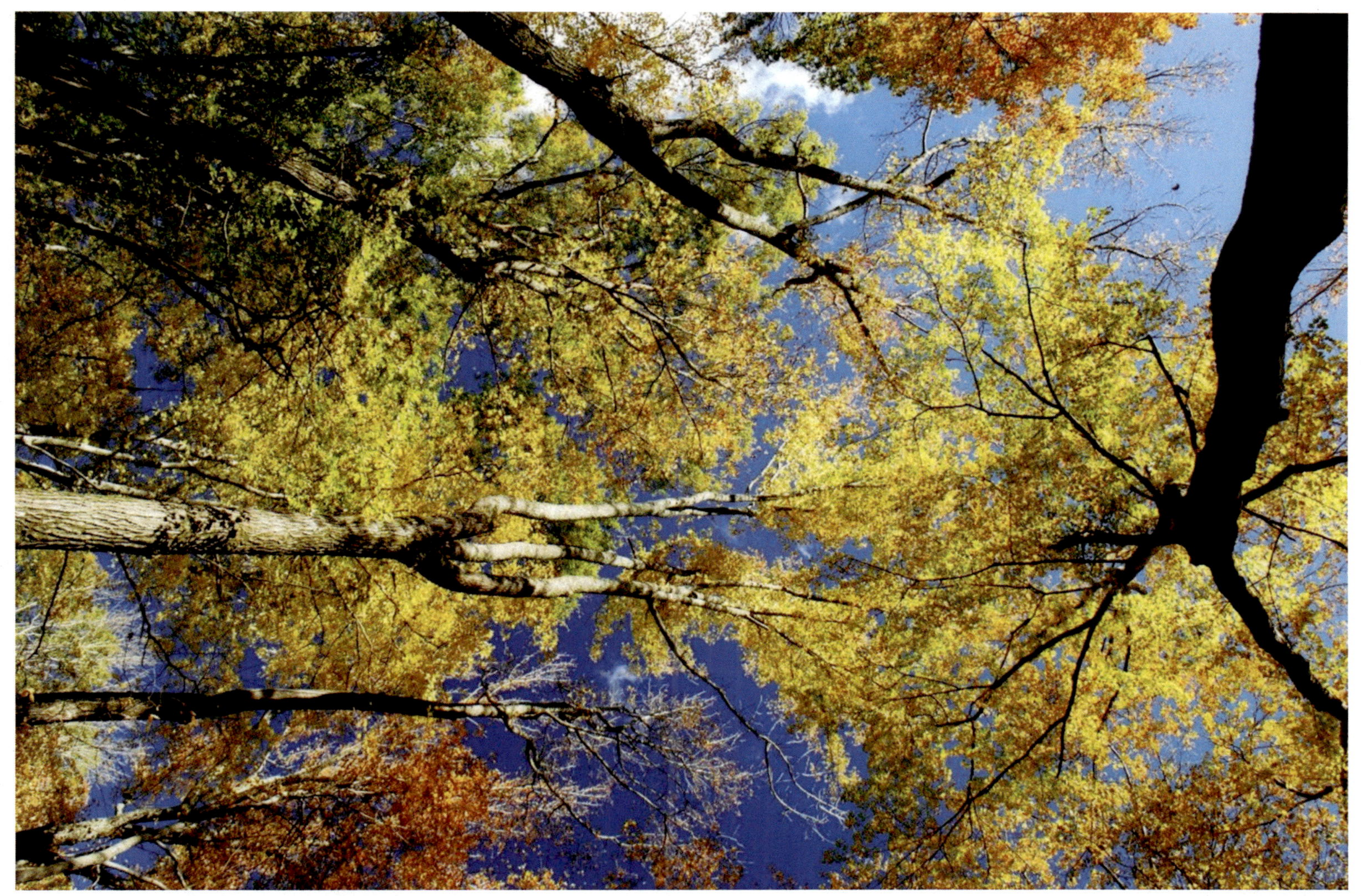

22. Trees flaunt their fire during this glorious but all-too short peak fall season.

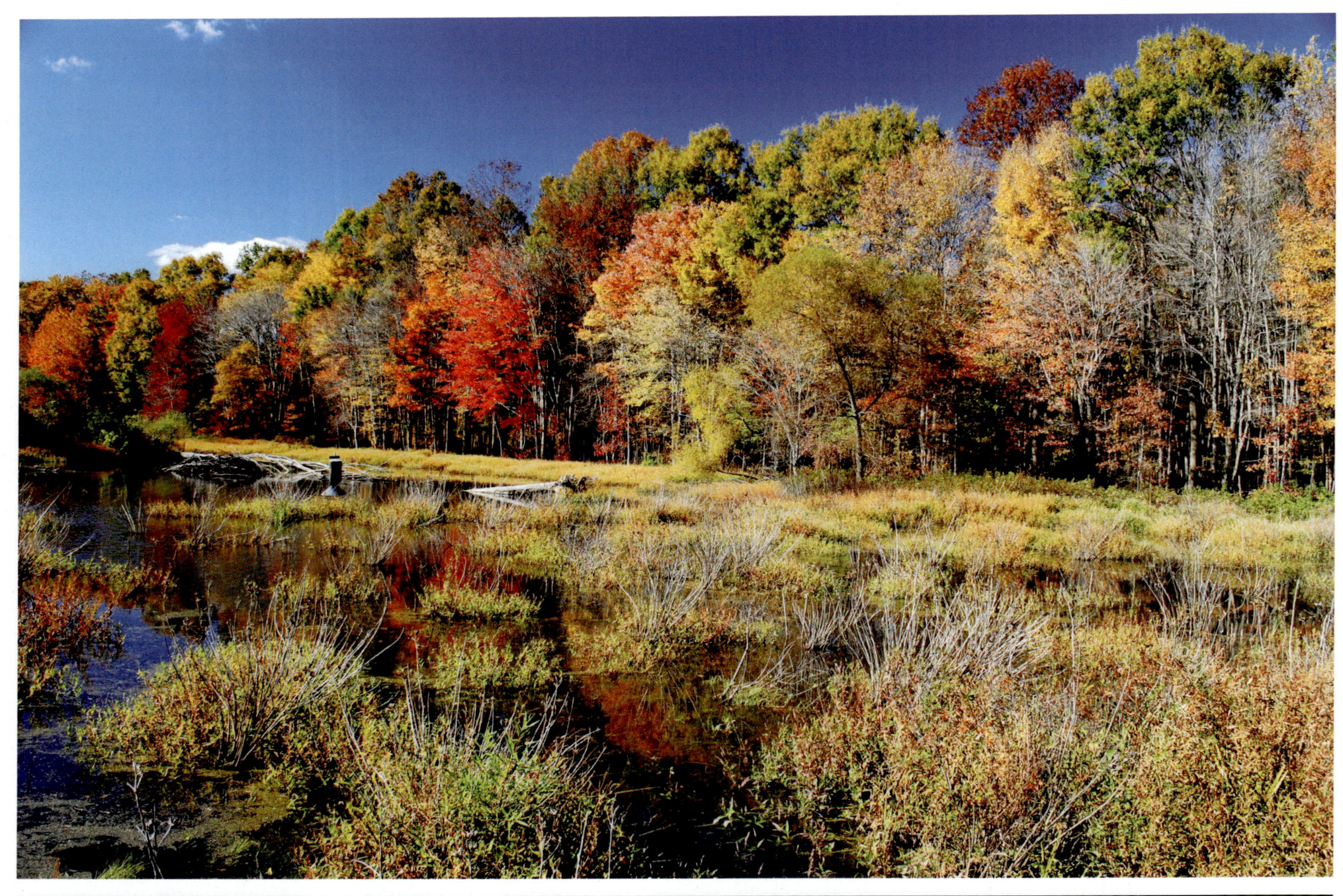

23. "There is harmony in autumn, and a lustre in its sky." ~ Percy Bysshe Shelley

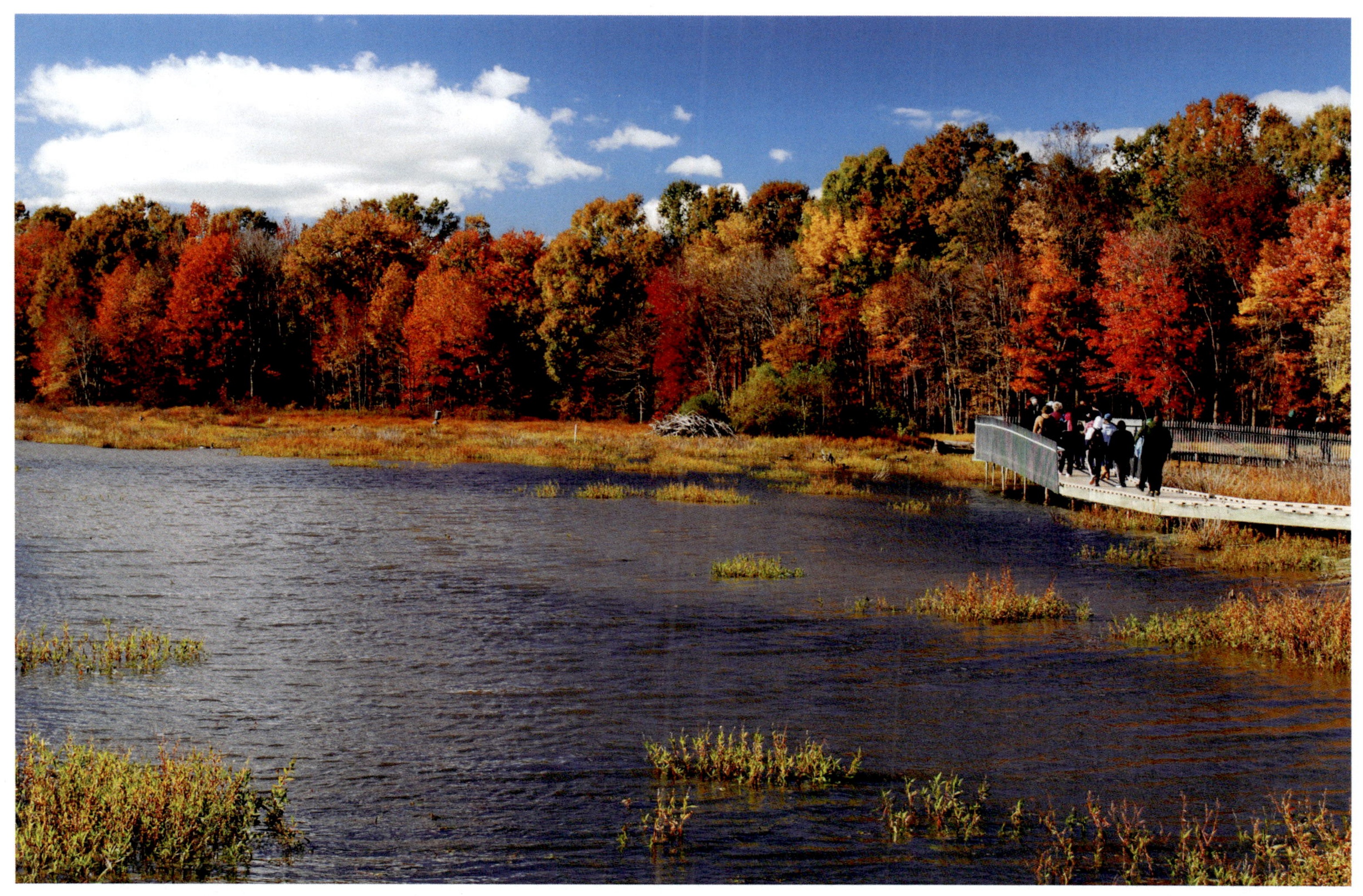

24. The convergence of bright sun and robust color make a Huntley Meadows' autumn a serious destination.

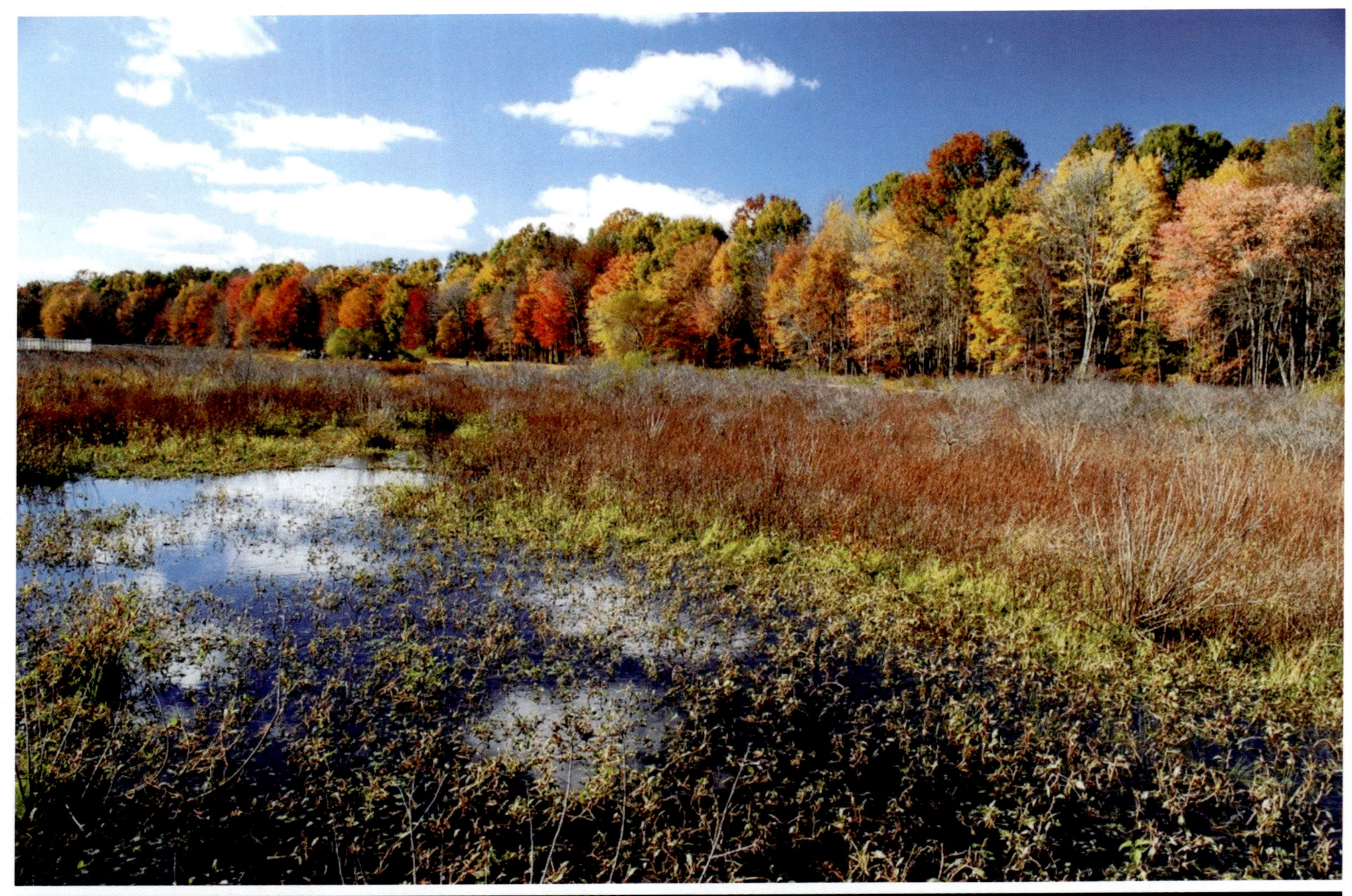

25. The wetlands in fall. Comfortable temperatures with impressive colors brings out painters as well as photographers.

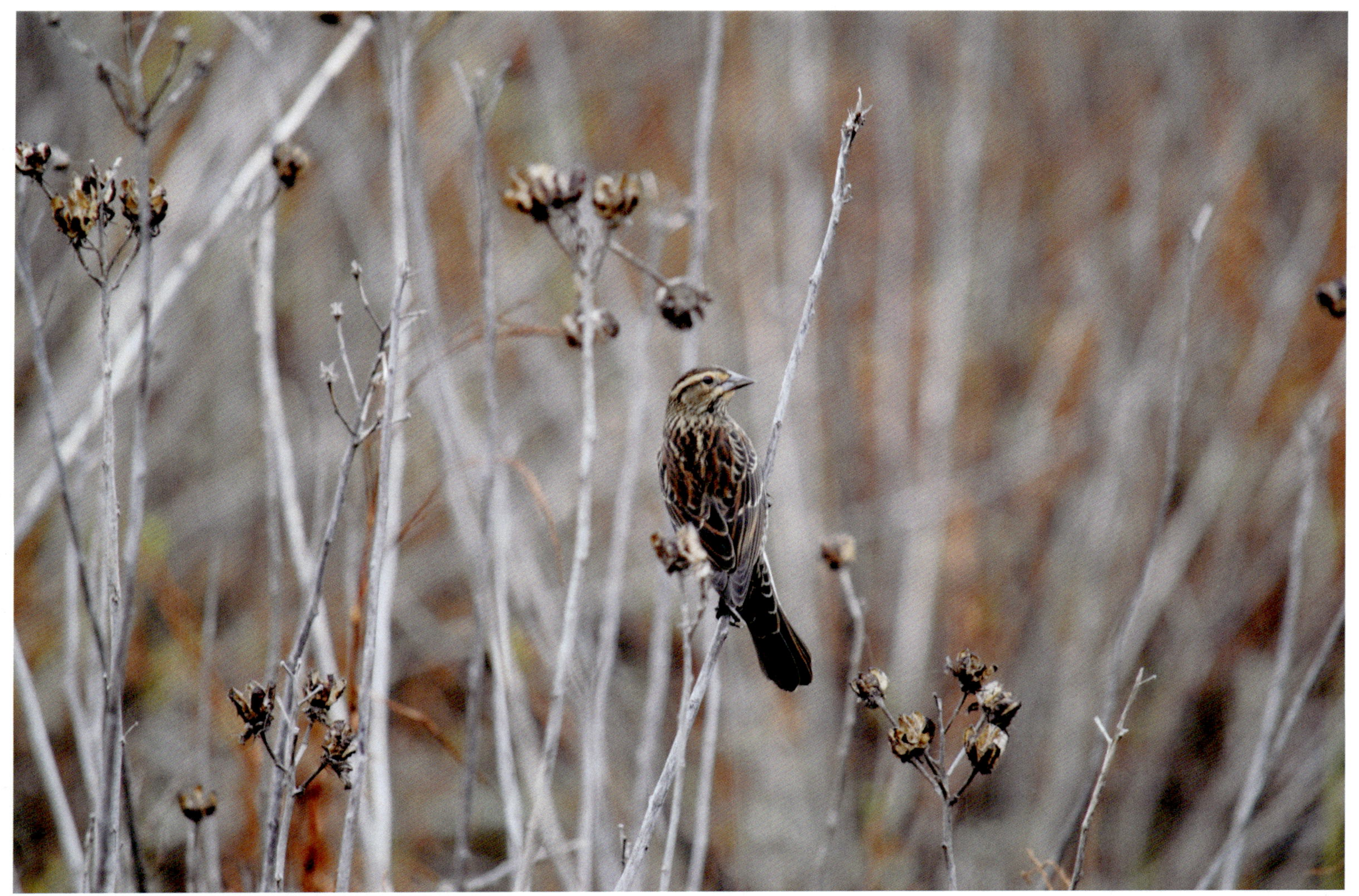

26. The red-winged blackbird is abundant nationwide and commonly seen throughout Huntley Meadows. Resting alertly is a female, shown here.

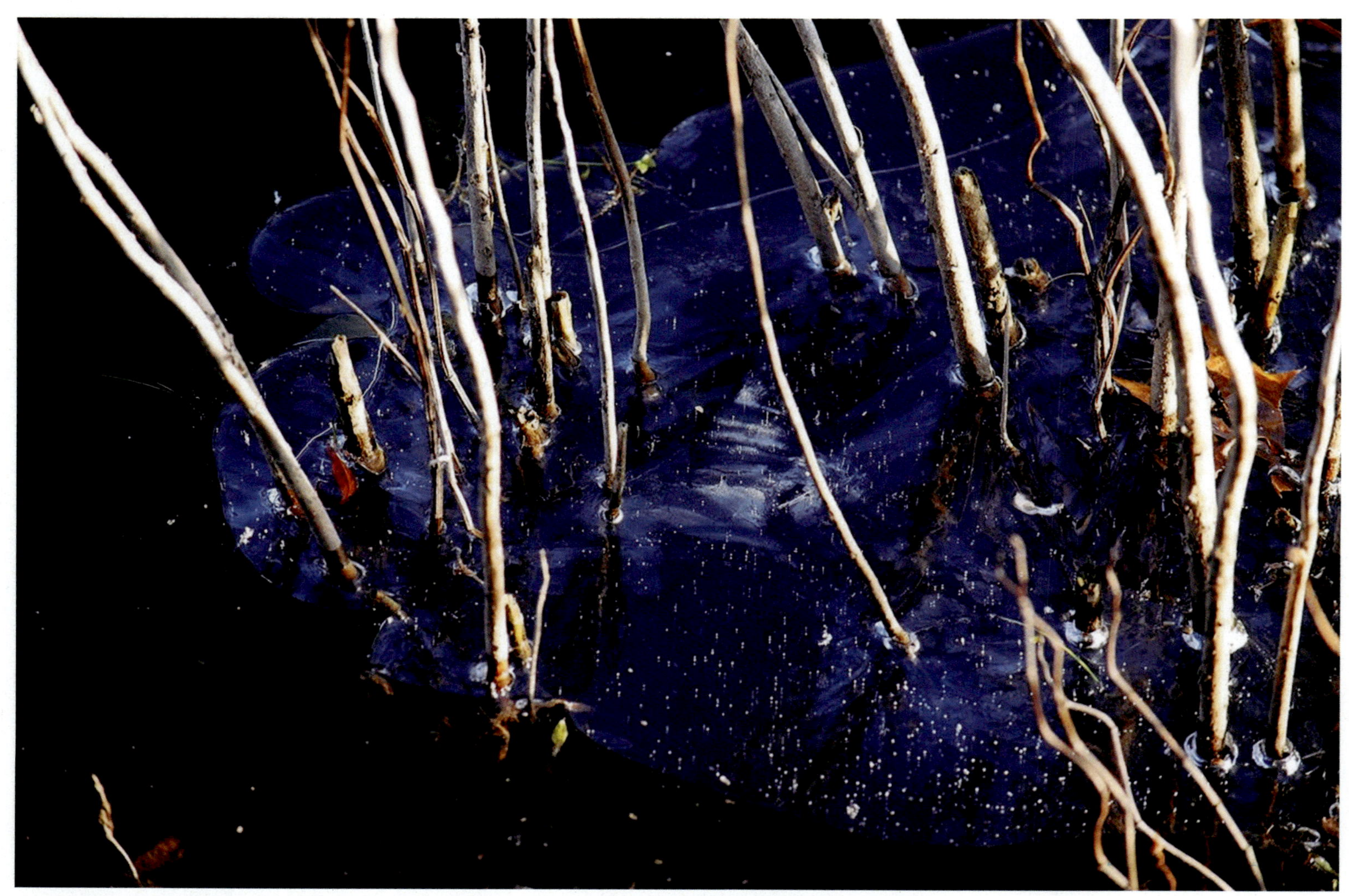

27. With the first light freeze in early fall, thin, colorful ice patches appear.

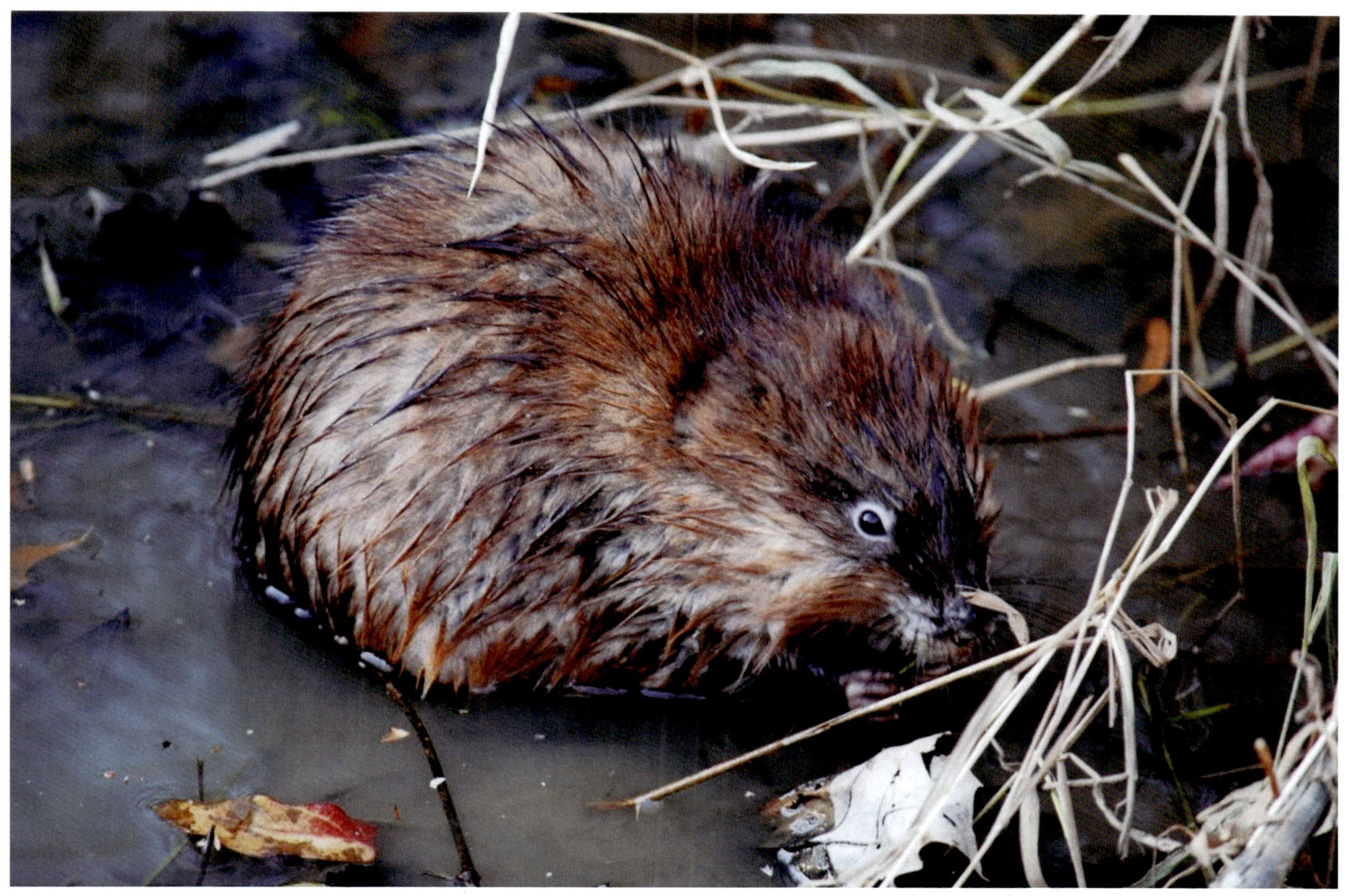

28. A muskrat, which is smaller than a beaver, feeds in this landscape. They thrive in aquatic environments like Huntley Meadows. Muskrats can survive underwater for as long as 20 minutes and even can swim backwards.

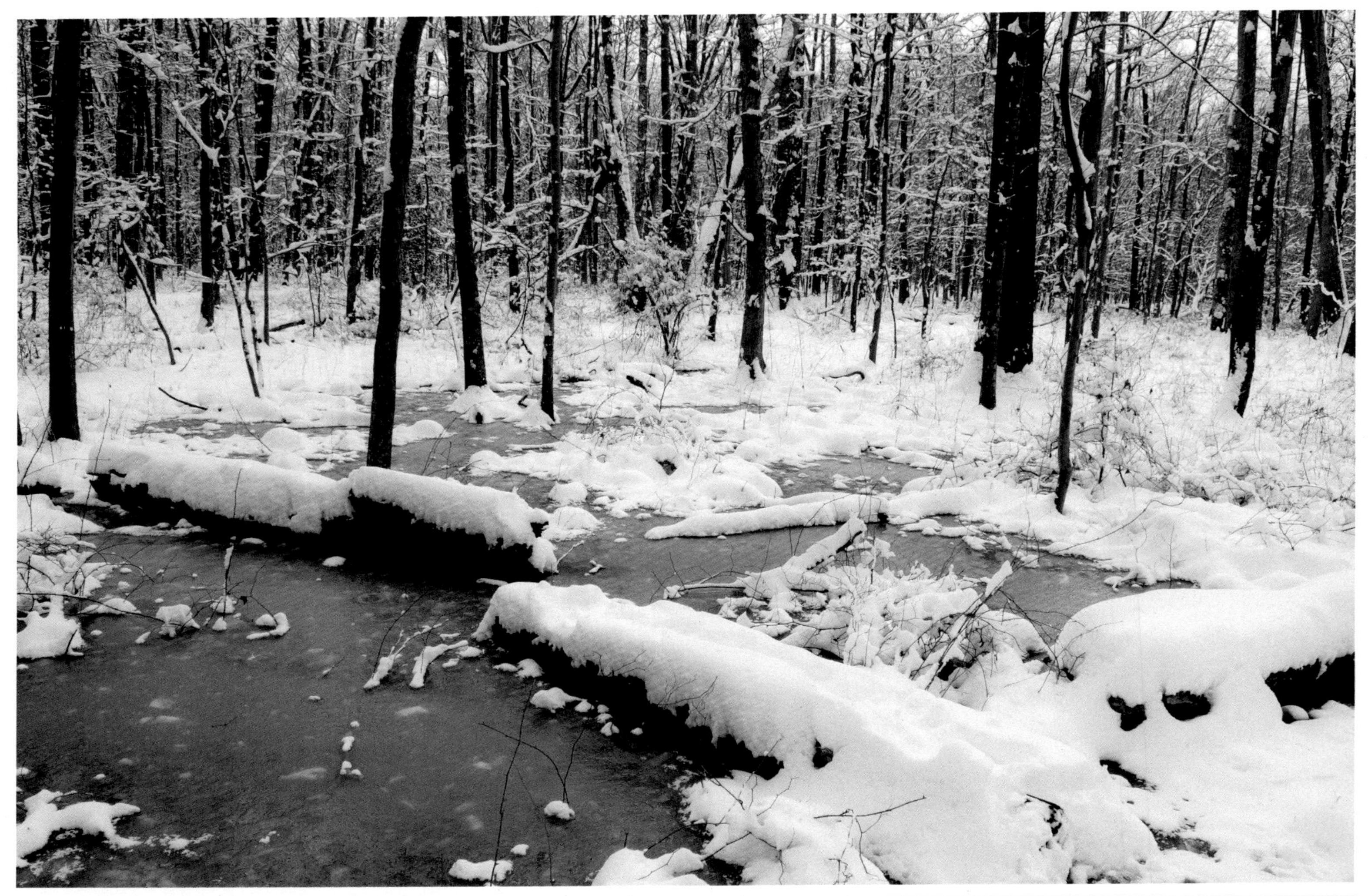

29. "Chill airs and wintry winds! my ear Has grown familiar with your song;
I hear it in the opening year, I listen, and it cheers me long." ~ Henry Wadsworth Longfellow

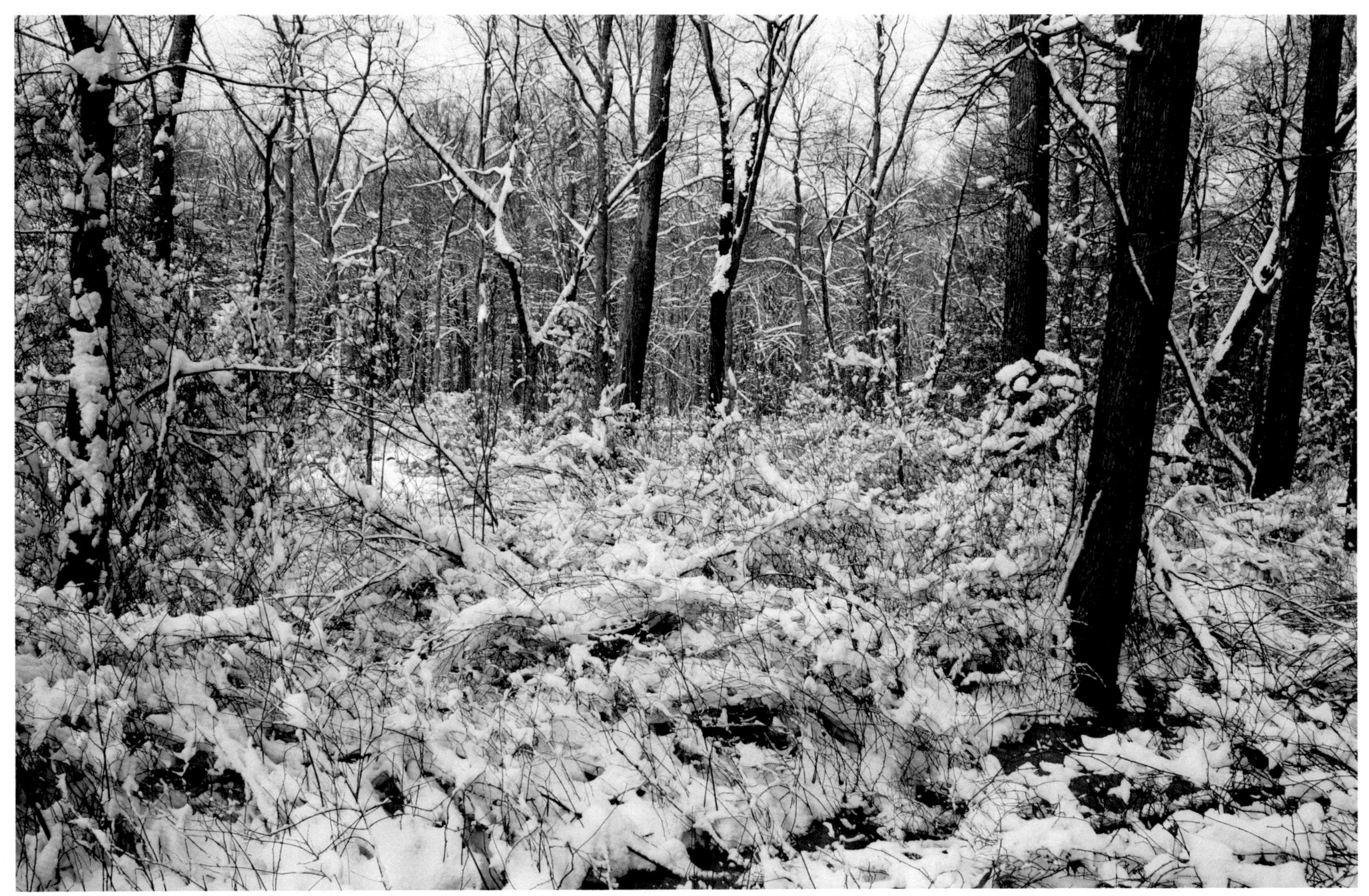

30. After a January snow, a morning that began with dark skies, brightened brilliantly by midday.

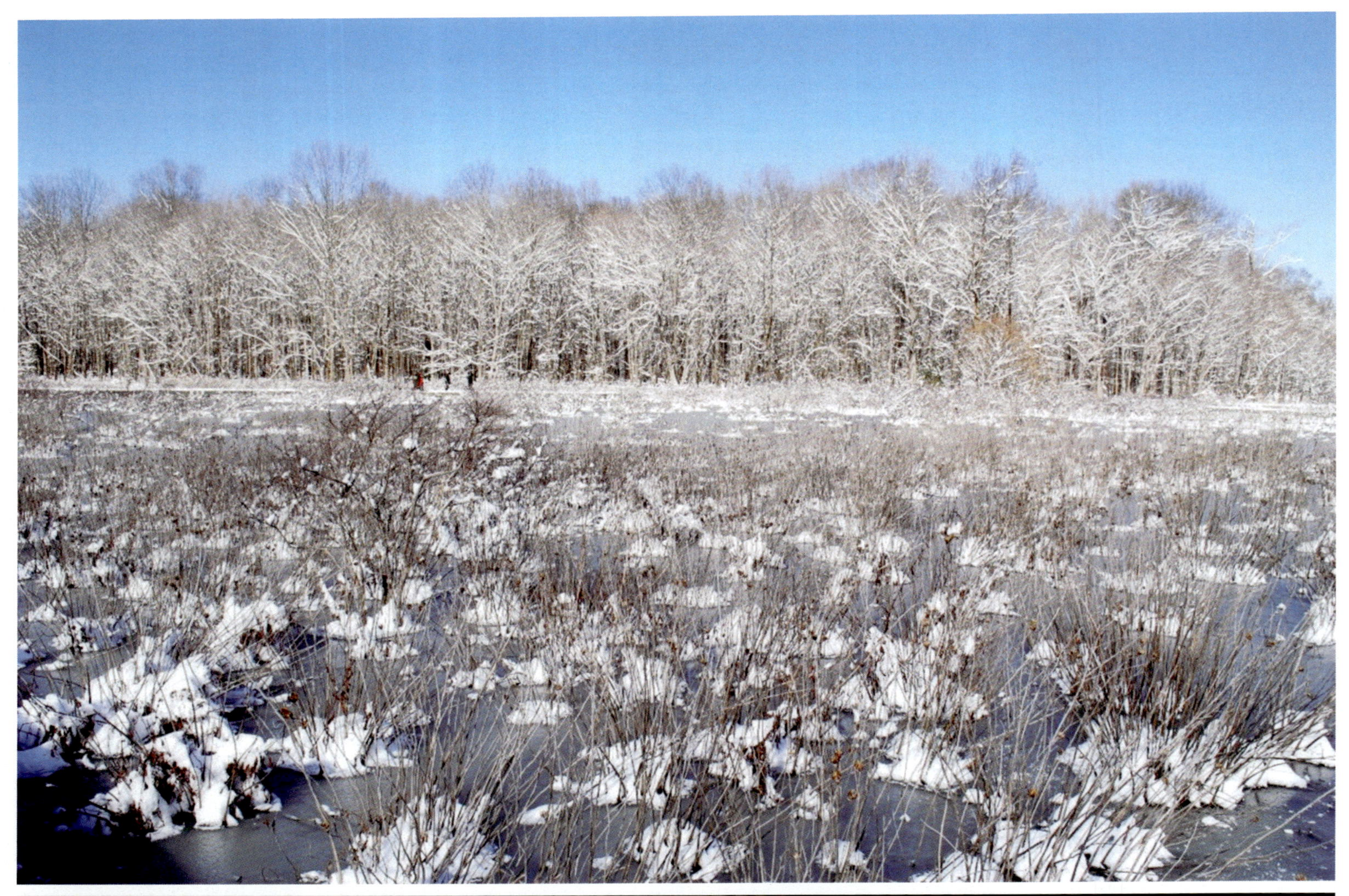

31. "The frolic architecture of the snow." ~ Ralph Waldo Emerson

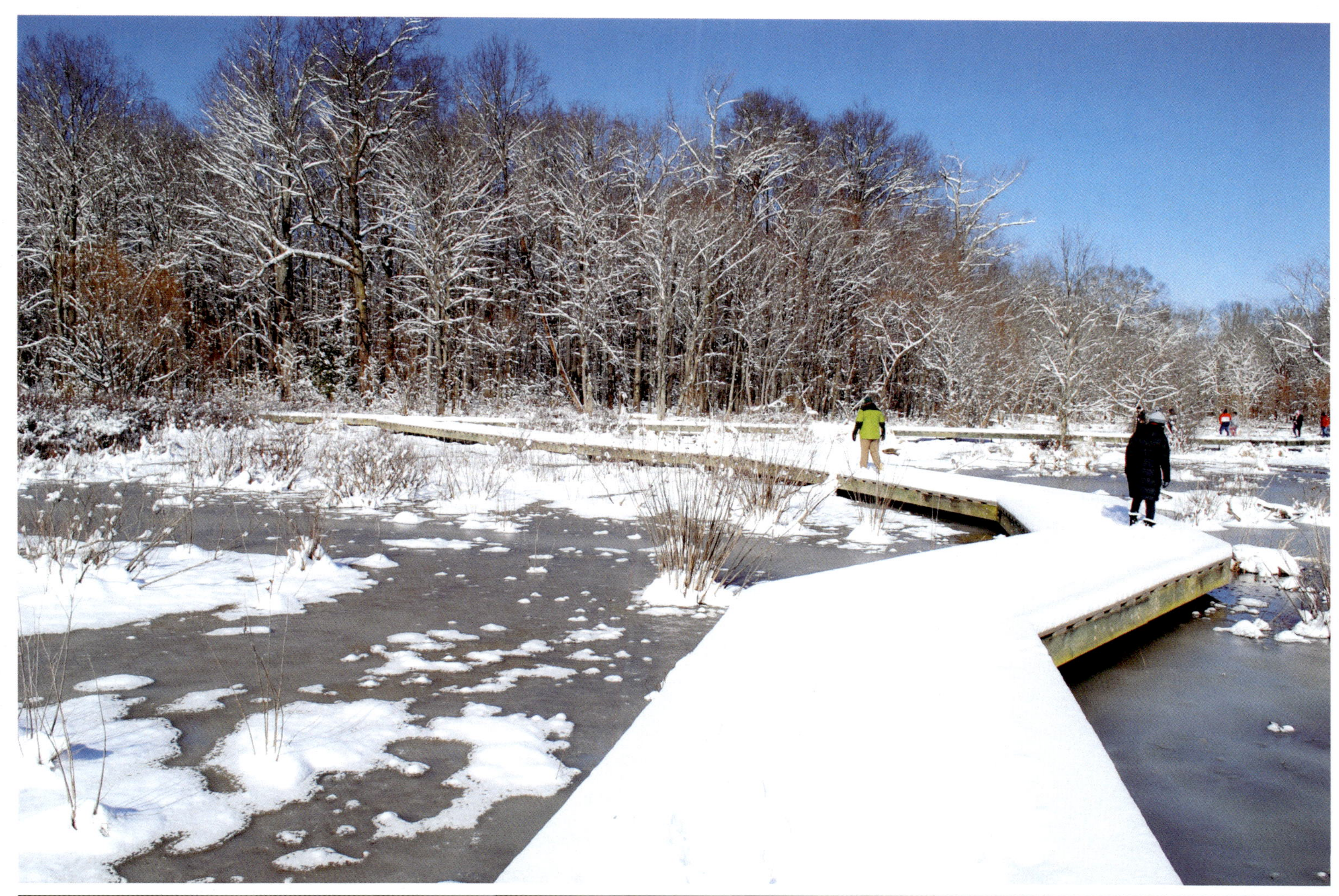

32. "I love the snow, and all the forms of the radiant frost." ~ Percy Bysshe Shelley

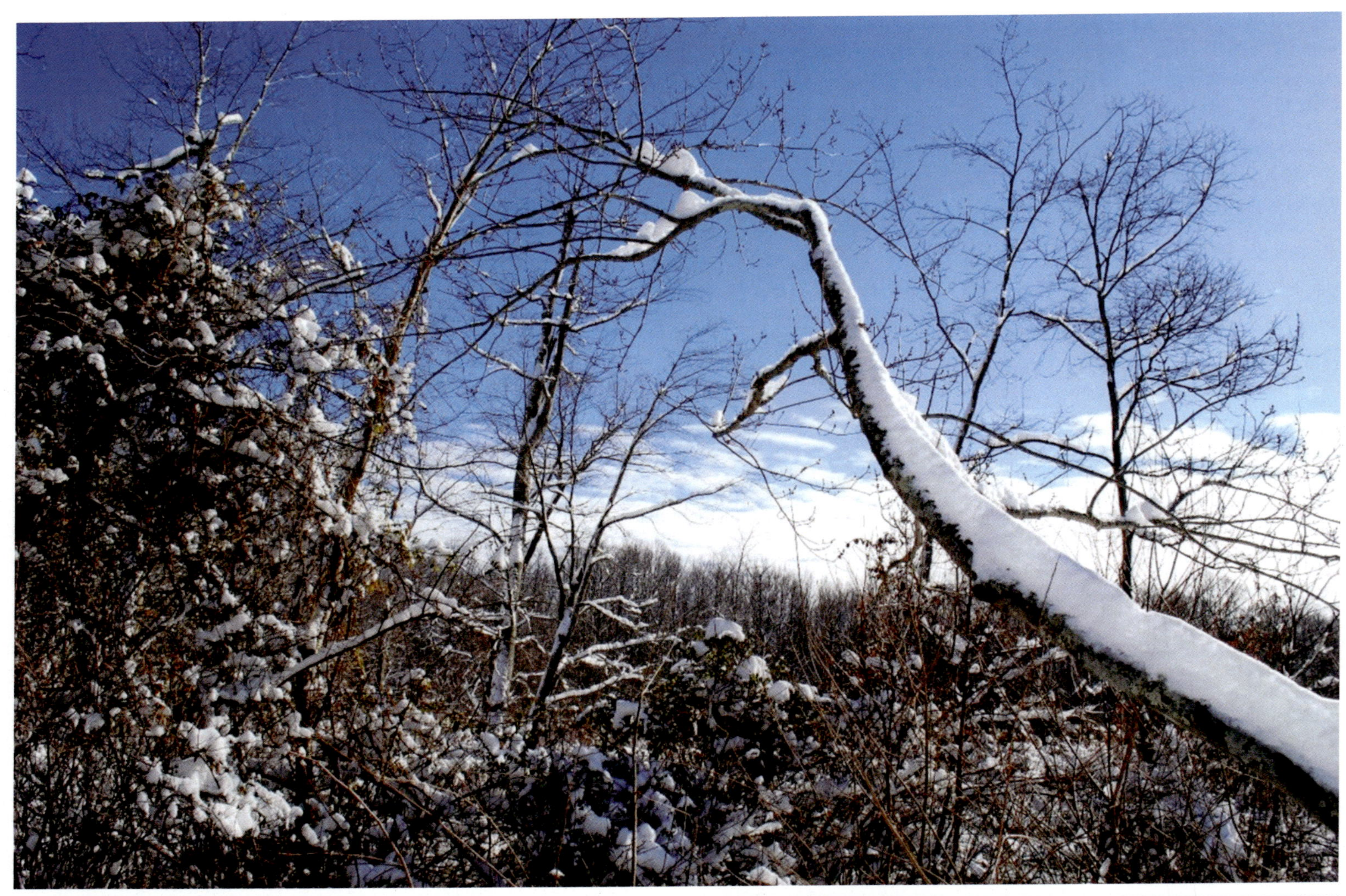

33. Snow makes an impression on every extended branch in Huntley Meadows.

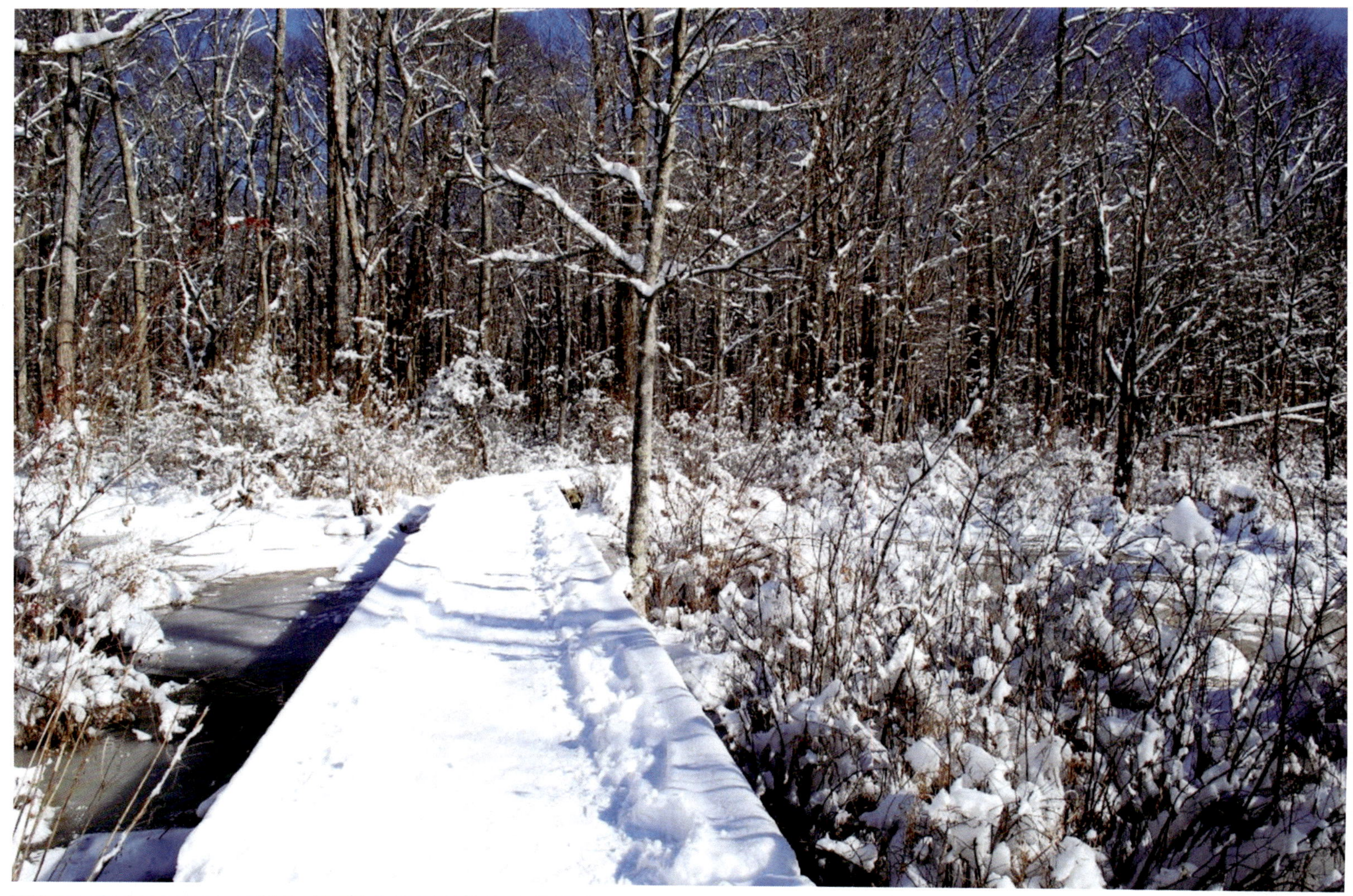

34. The boardwalk, a primary artery of the wetlands, under snow.

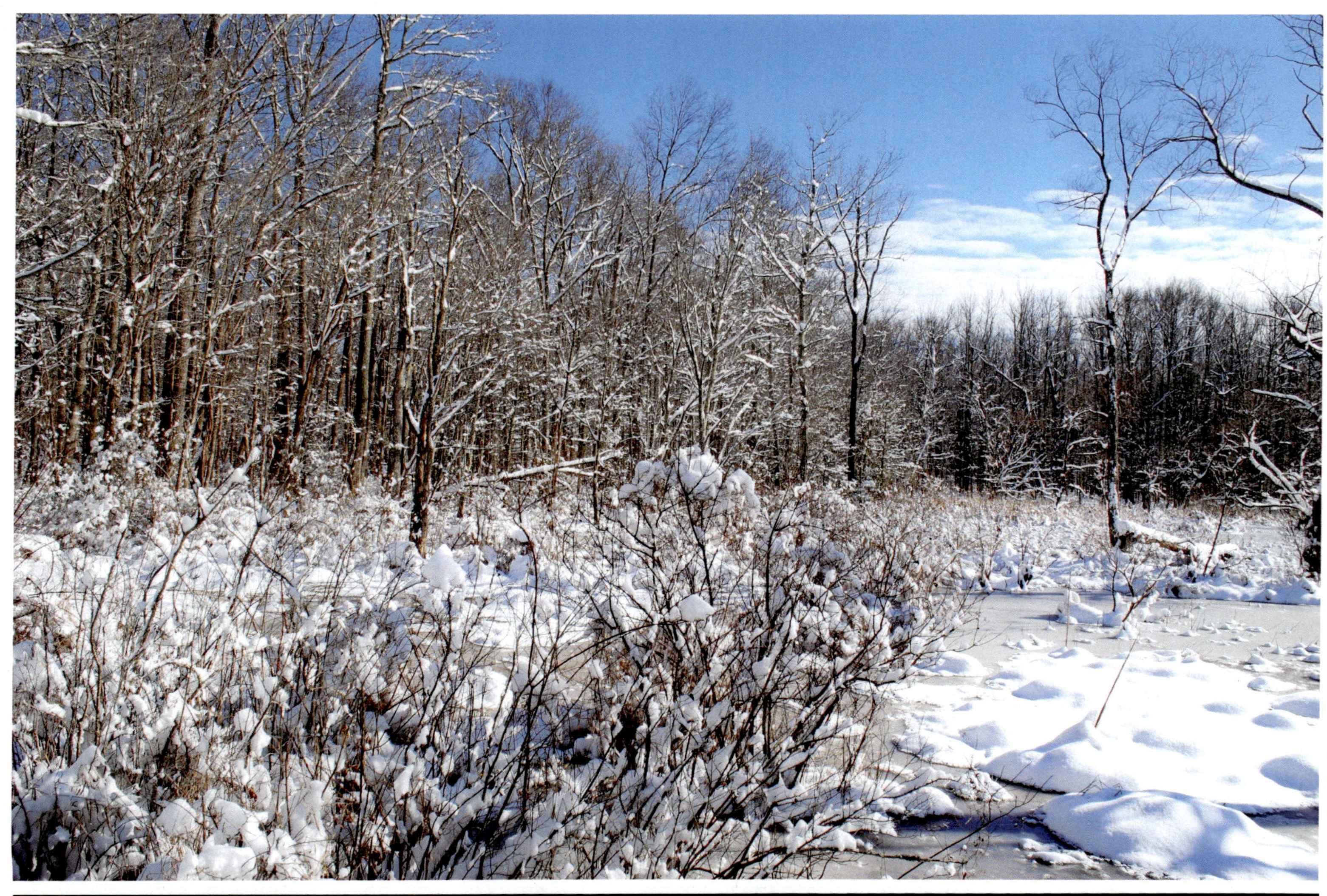

35. This major snow event renders the wetlands silent.

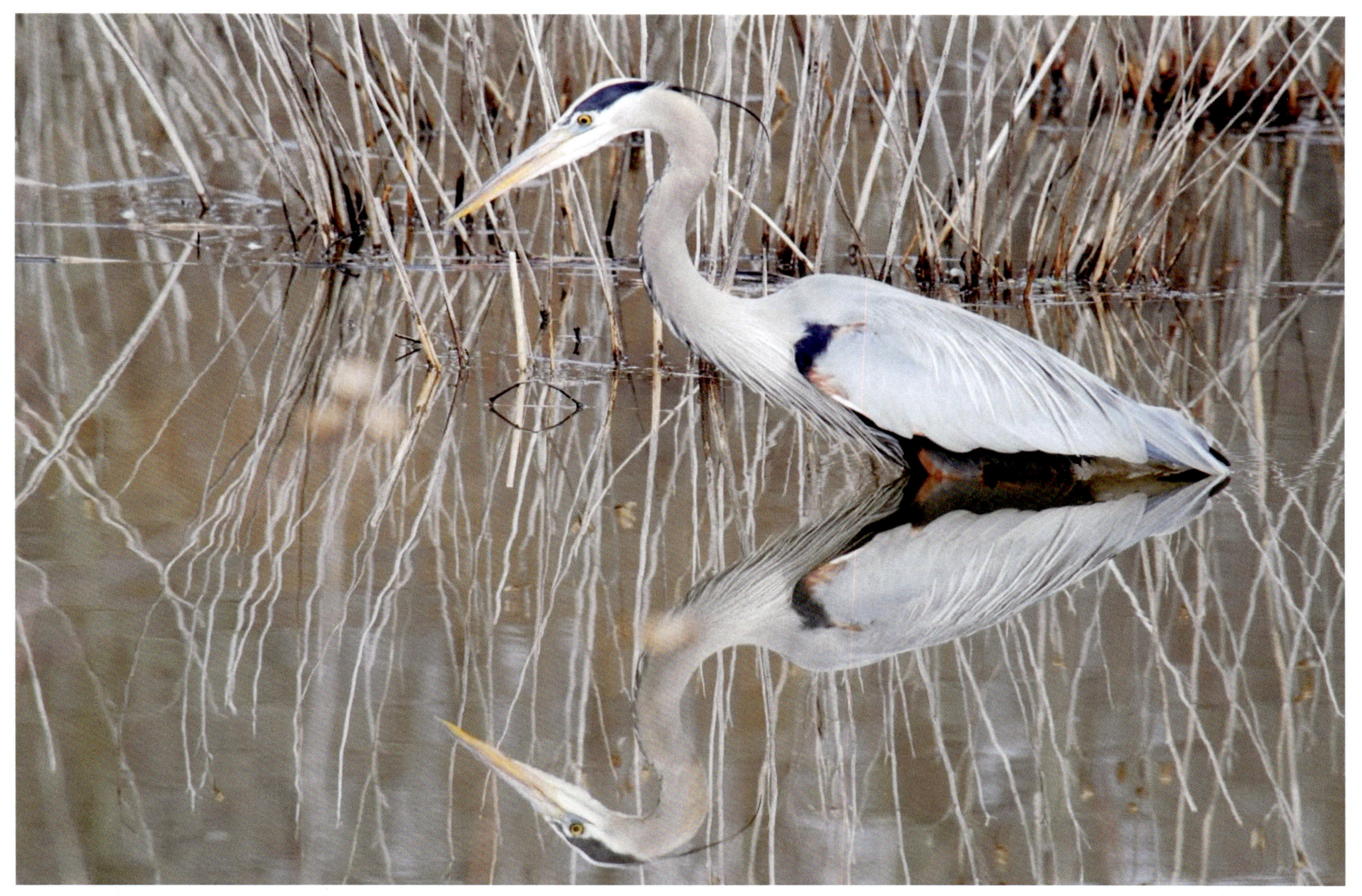

36. Spotting a great blue heron during February is a treat since they are known to migrate as far south as the tropics in the winter.

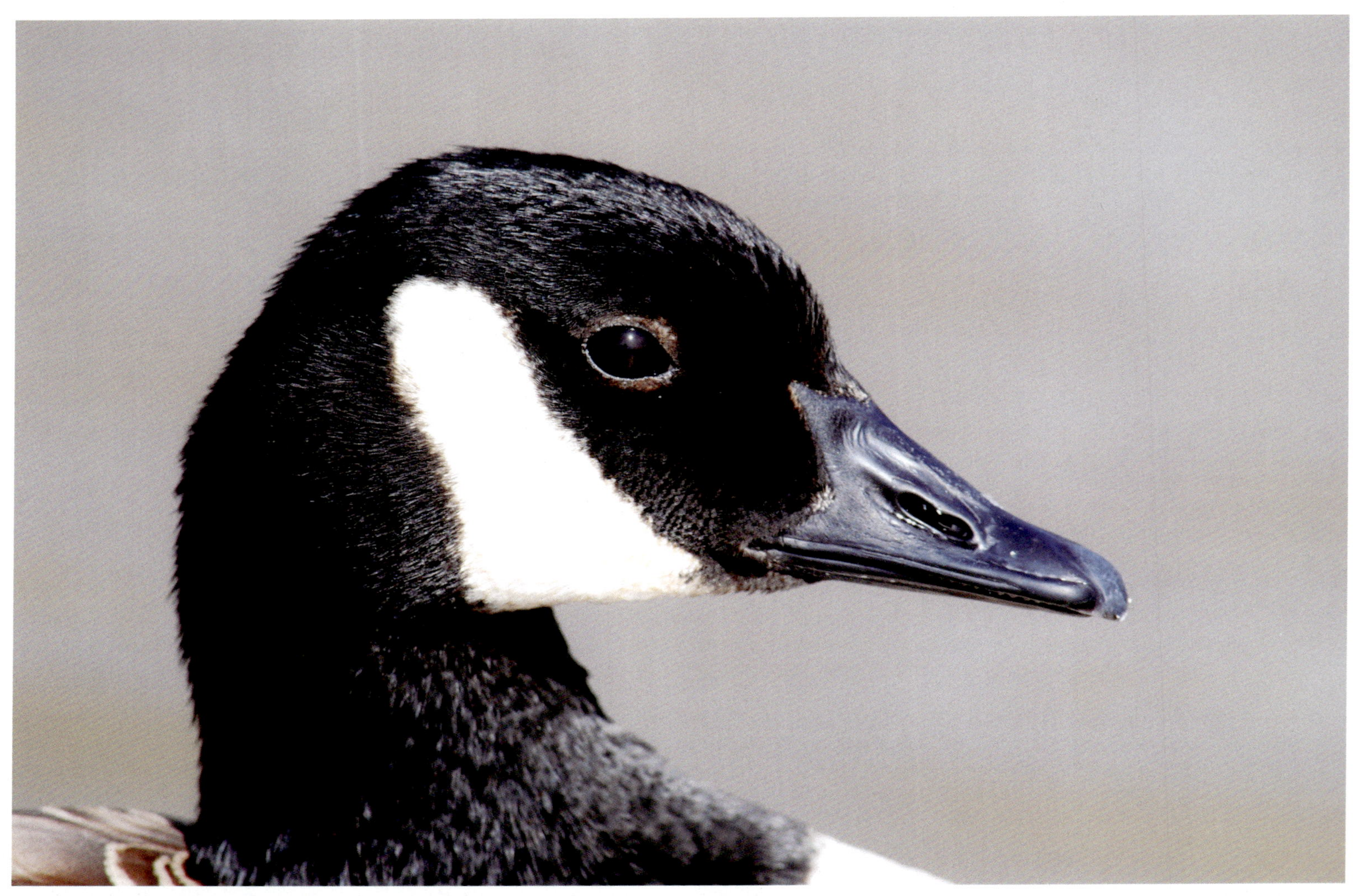

37. This patient, social Canada goose allowed me a closeup on the boardwalk. I noticed that my reflection is visible in its eye.

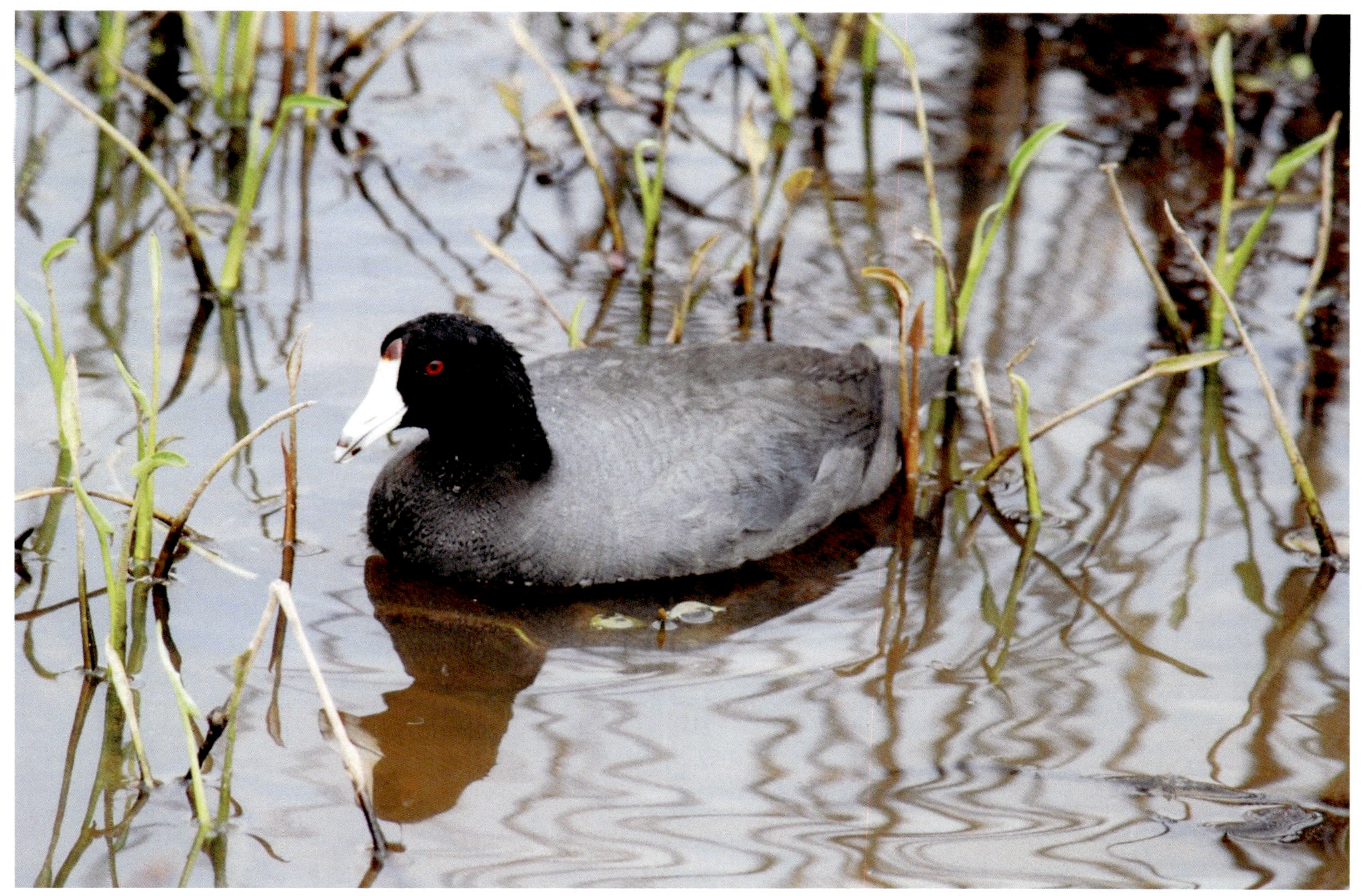

38. The American coot, a member of the rail family, resembles a duck. Their flexible, lobed toes make them effective swimmers and divers.

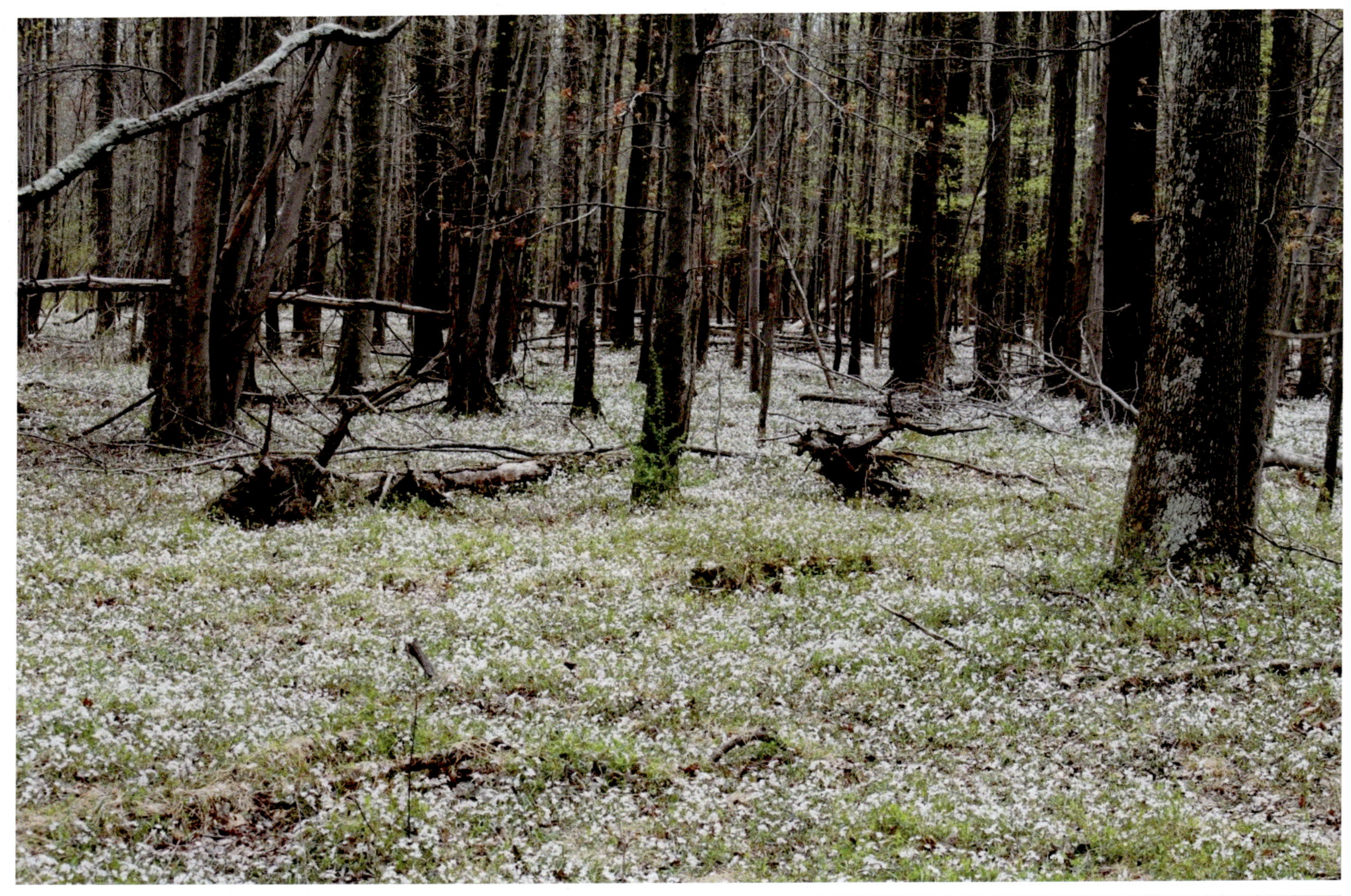

39. The profusion of spring beauties resembles a light snowfall on the forest floor. Also known as claytonia virginica, these native wildflowers have nectar that attracts various types of bees.

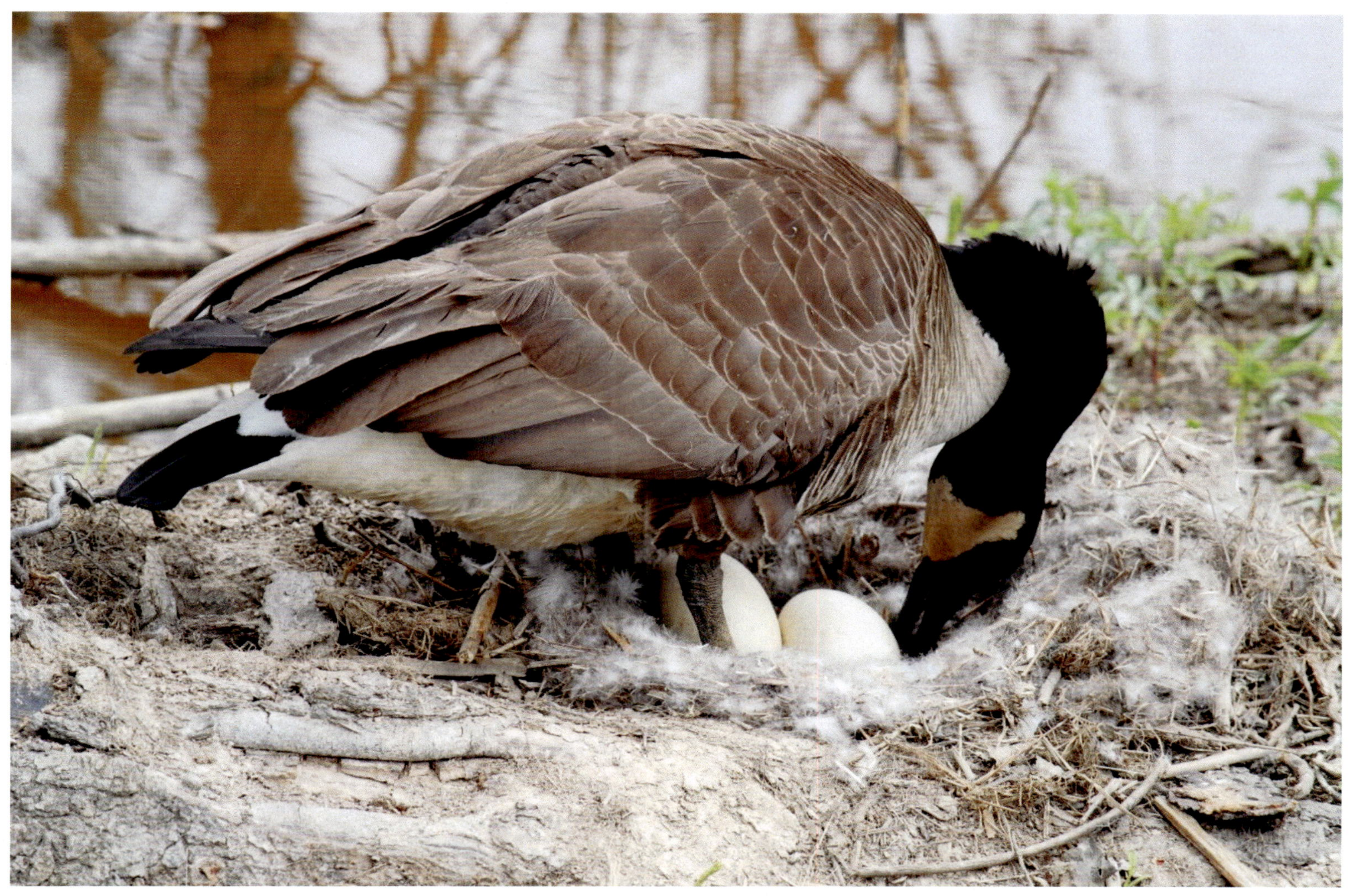

40. This Canada goose protects its eggs that rest in a nest of sticks, vegetation, and down from the female. The female incubates eggs for about a month while the male provides her food and protection.

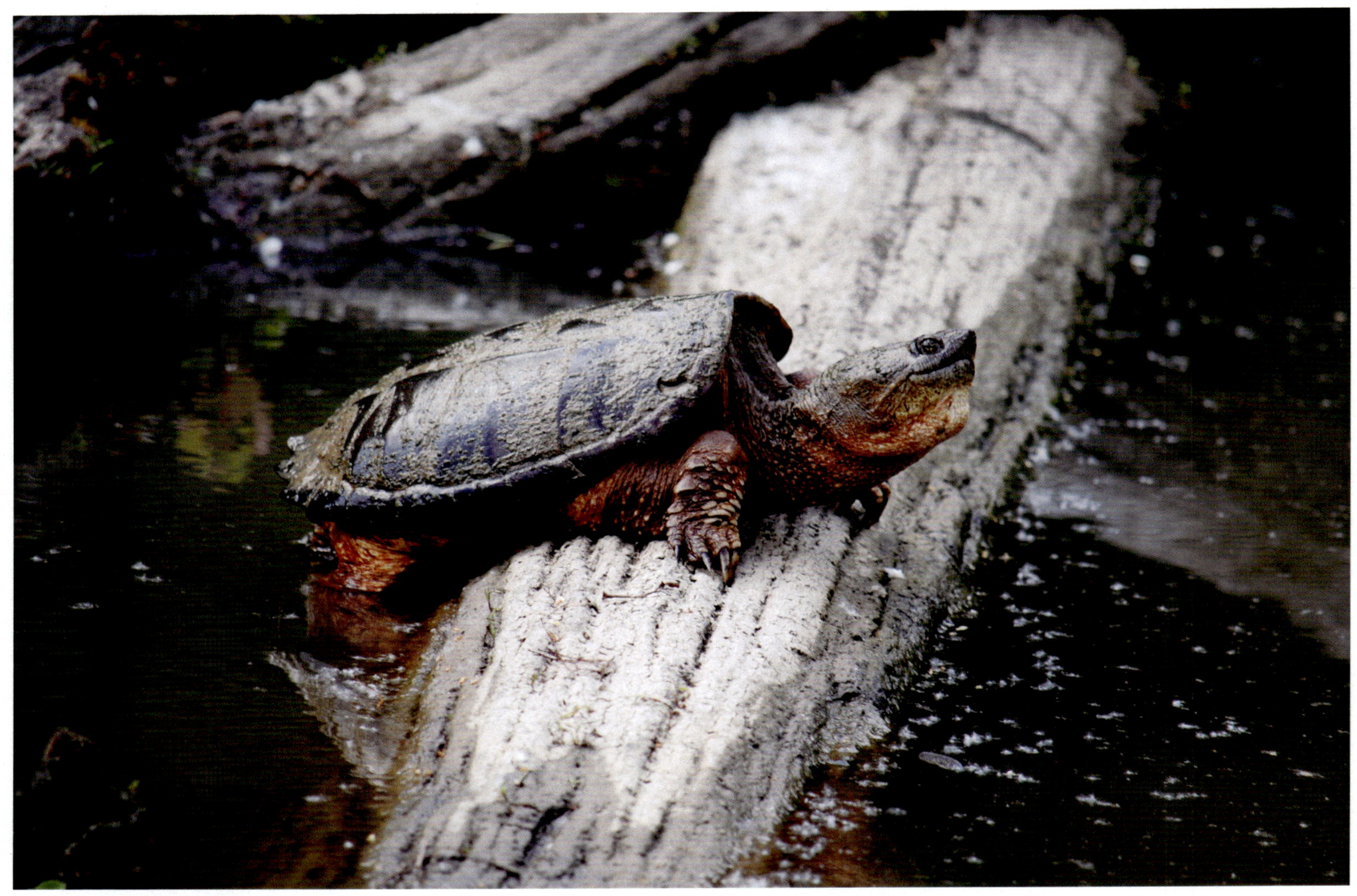

41. Powerful snapping turtles, like this one, are serious predators, devouring anything they can catch day or night. The largest turtles in Virginia, they can live up to 30 years.

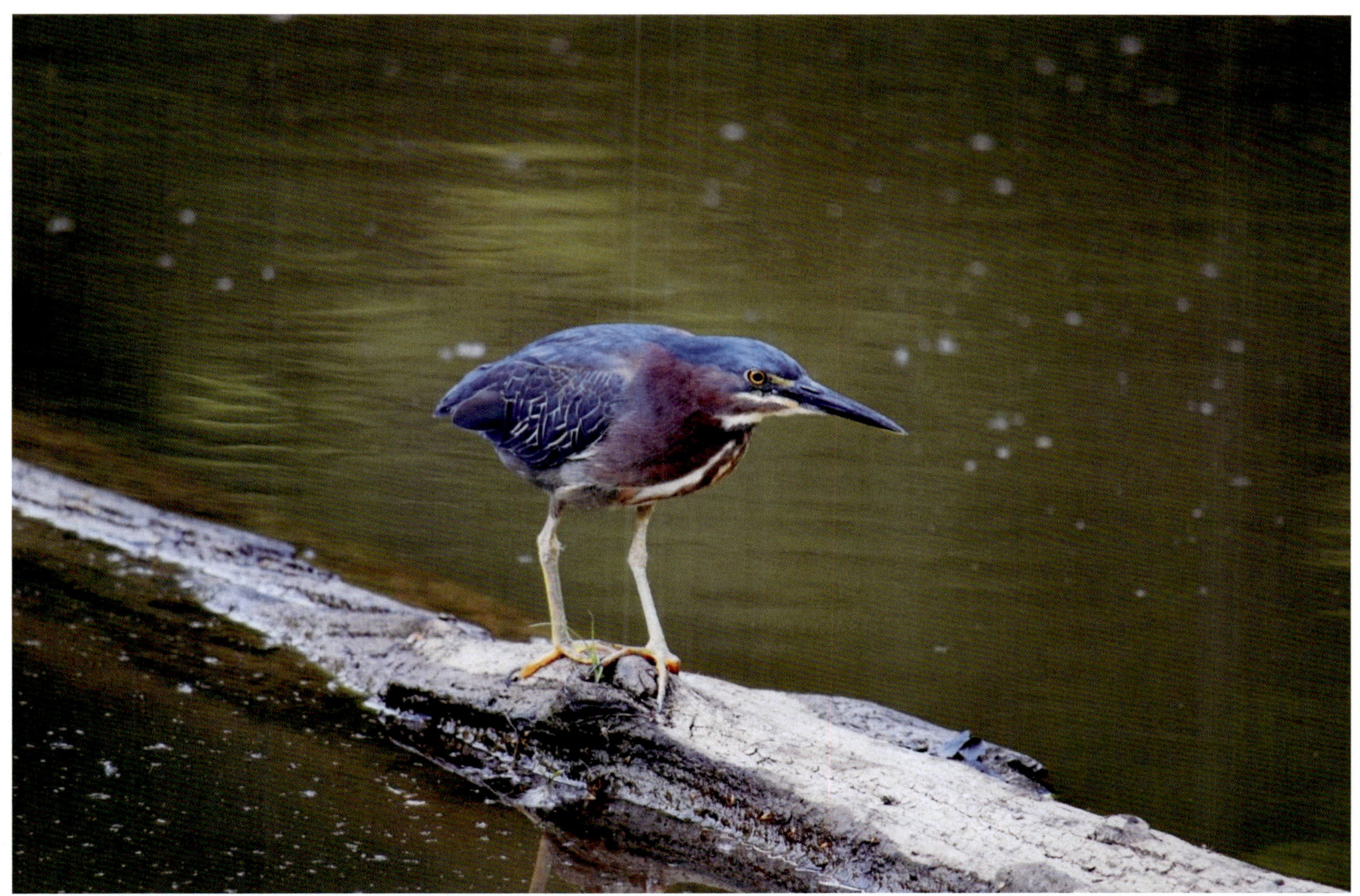

42. This curious green heron studies a snapping turtle on a nearby log.

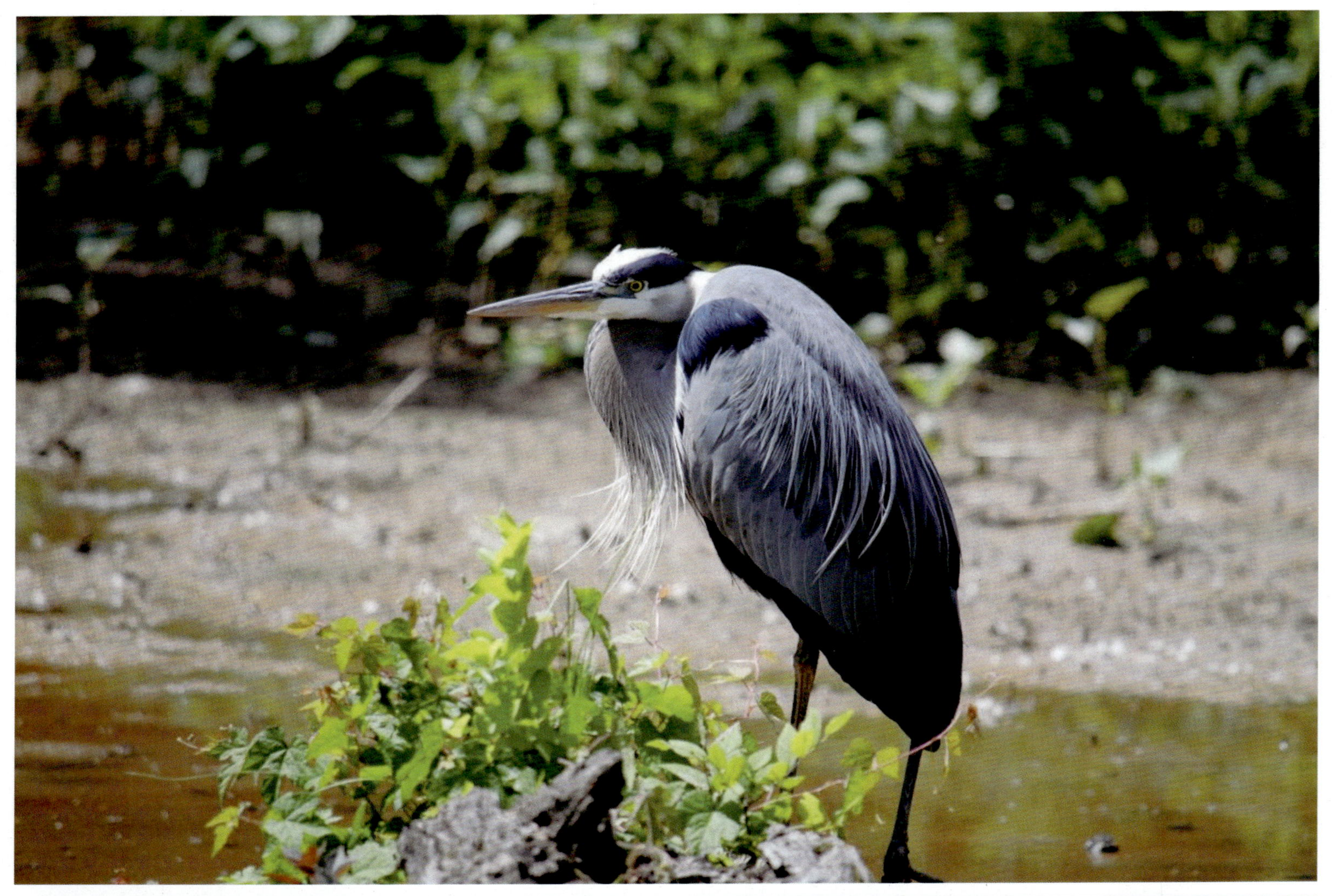

43. The great blue heron with its beautiful plumage is a joy to observe whether it's resting, hunting, or flying.

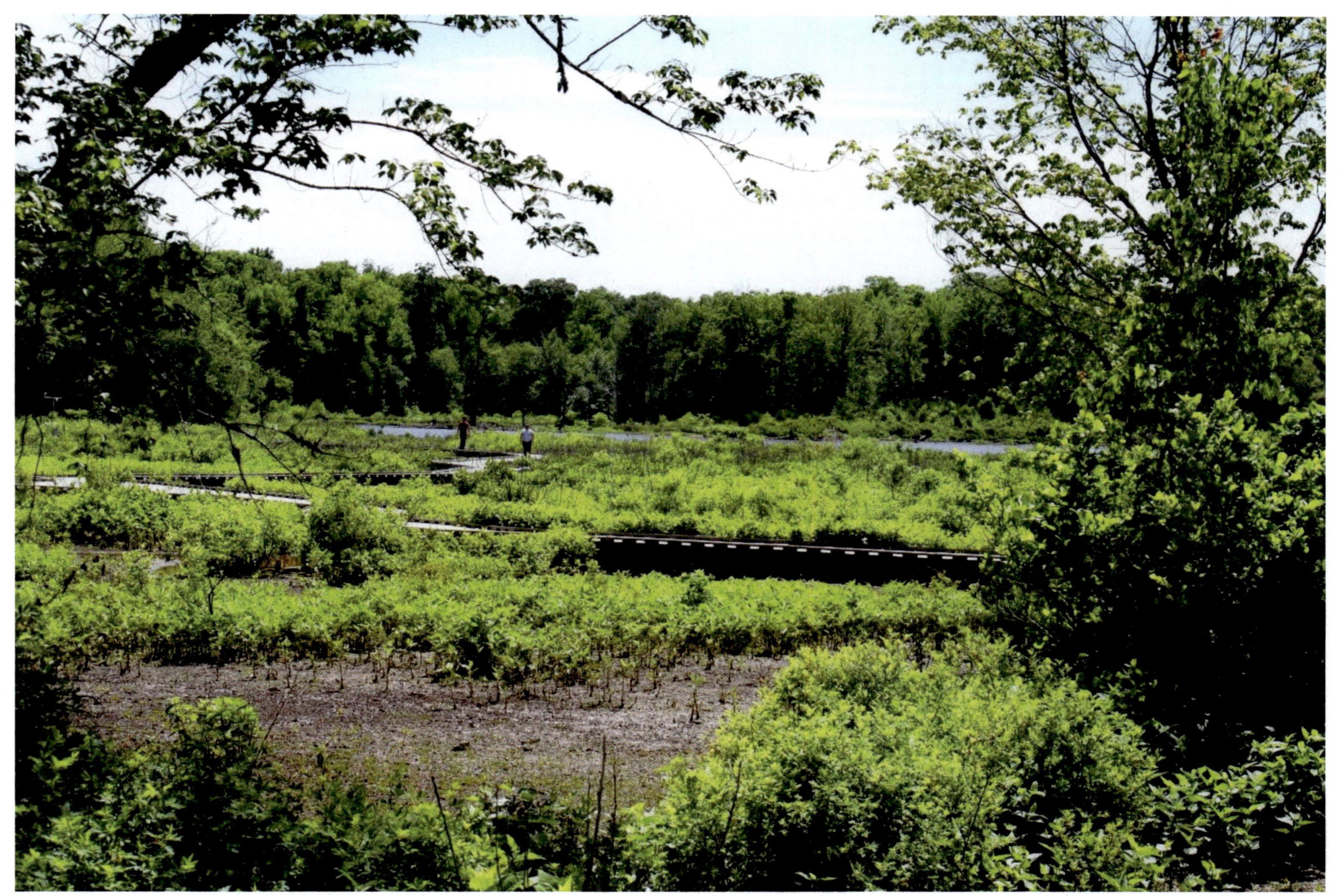

44. Spring warmth and rain can transform the park from dormant brown/grey to green in a few short weeks.

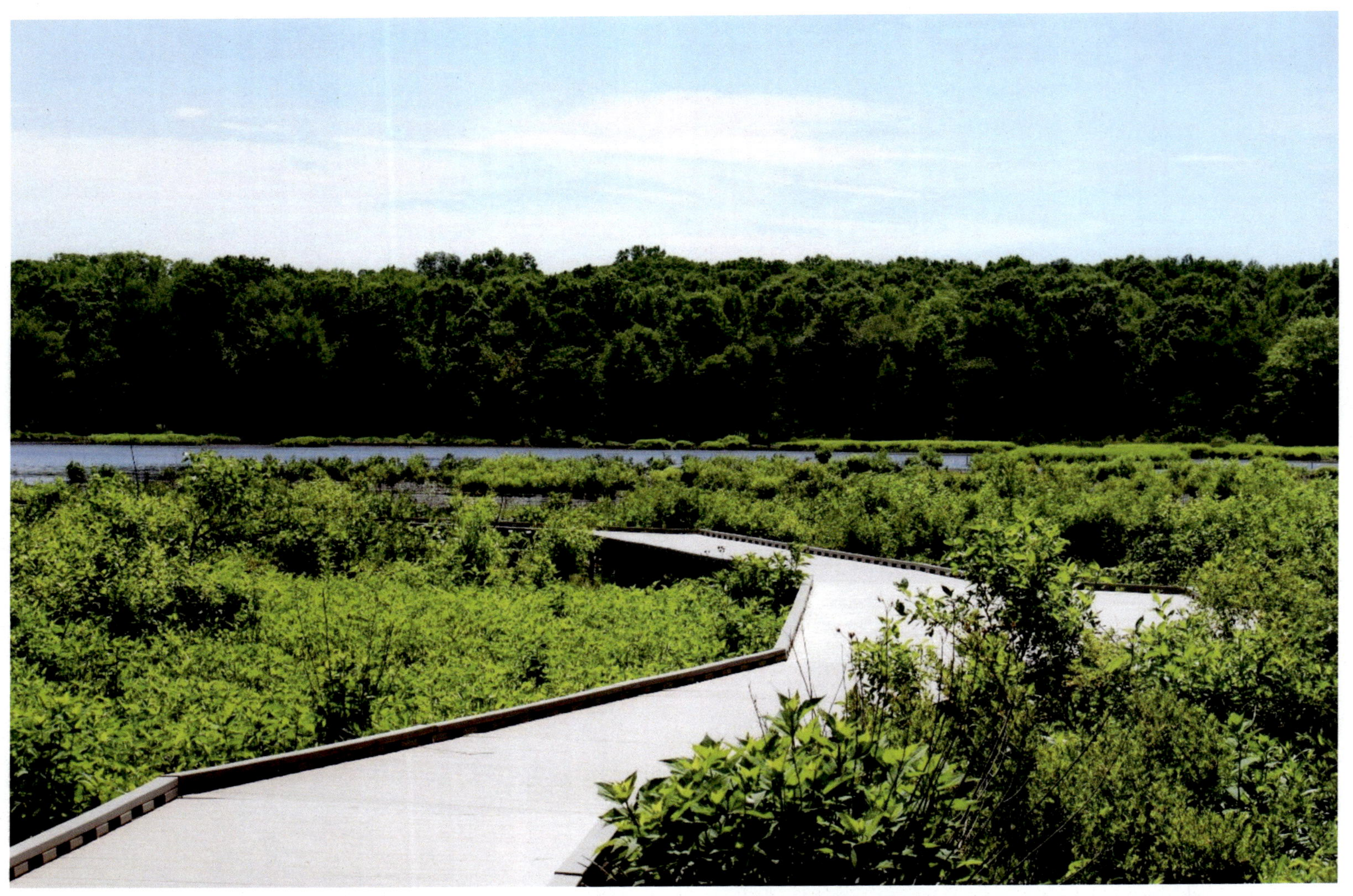

45. In spring, the boardwalk beckons visitors into the middle of the fragrant and blossoming marsh.

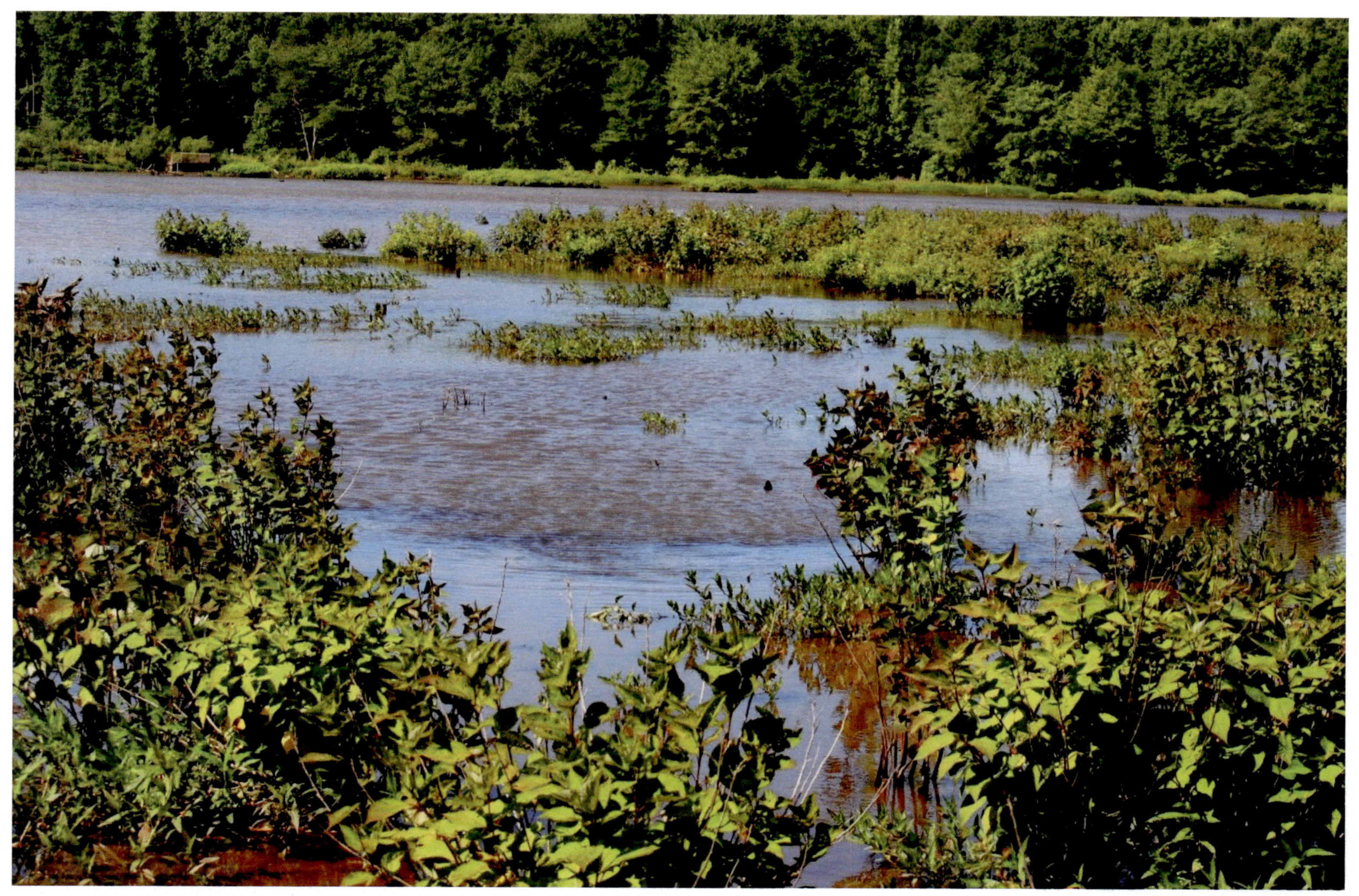

46. In just this small section of the wetlands, an immeasurable amount of plant, aquatic, and animal life thrive.

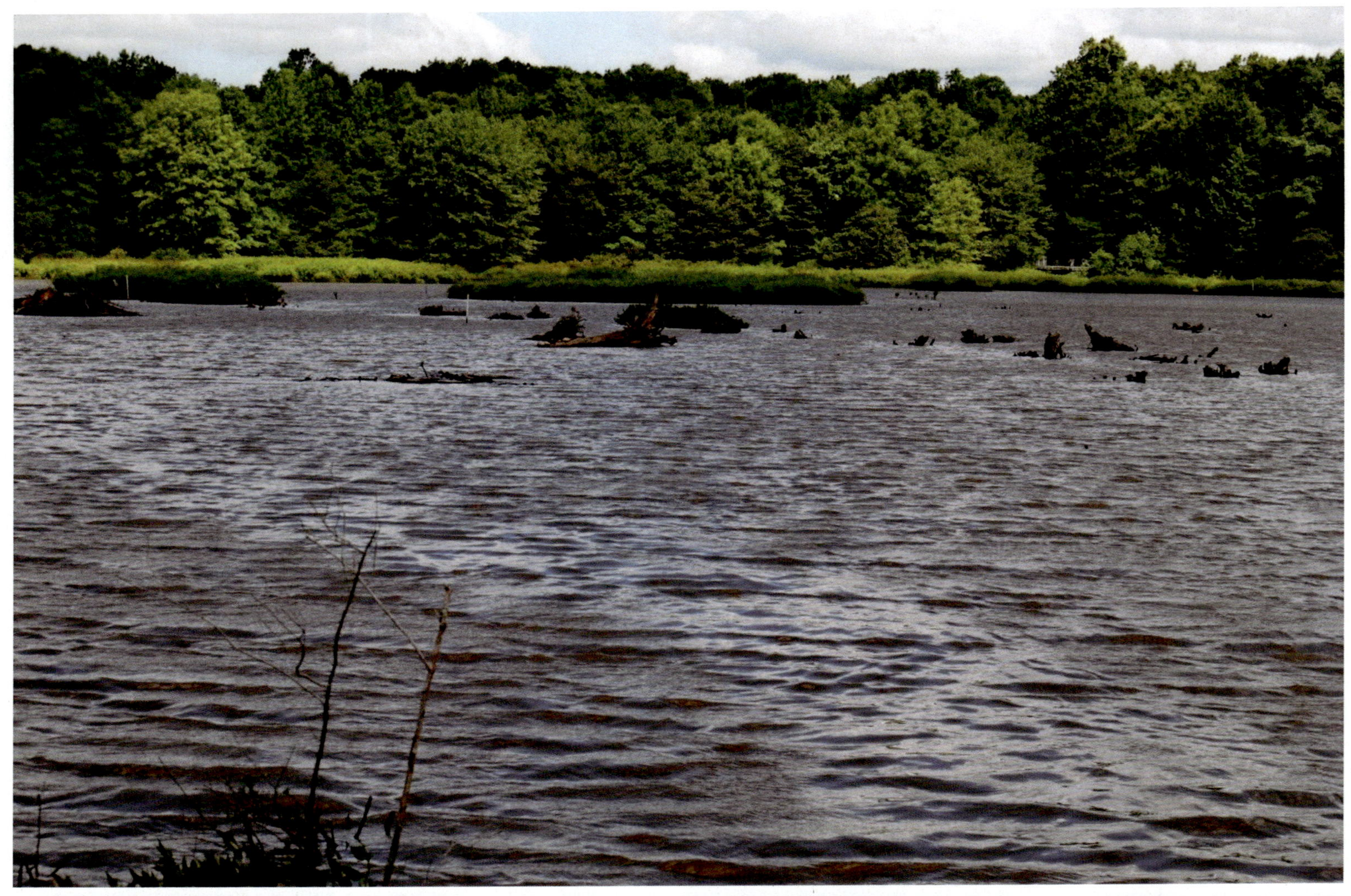

47. Adequate rainfall and careful water management ensures that Huntley Meadows remains a hemi-marsh, comprised of a proportional amount of water and vegetation.

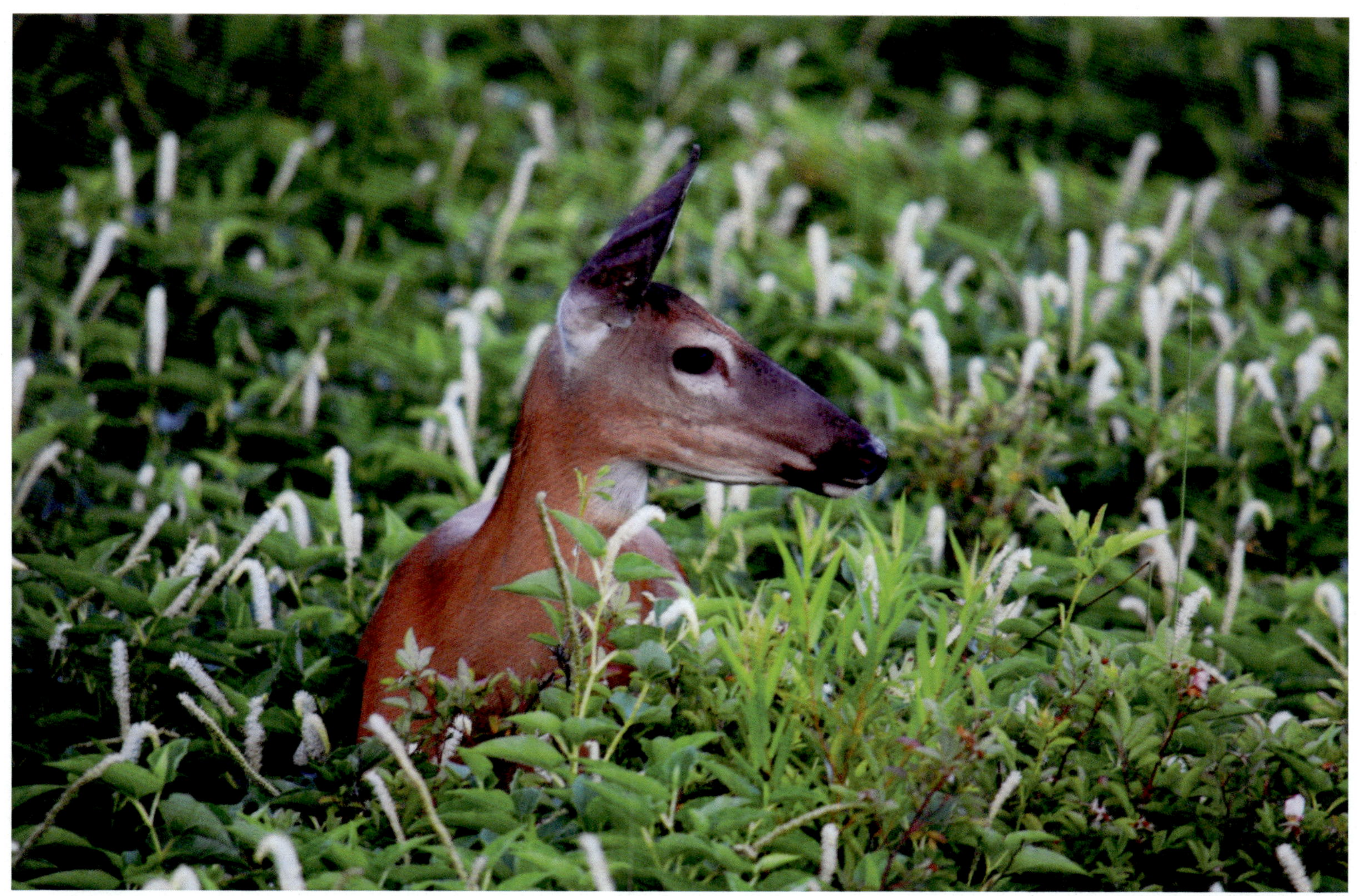

48. White-tailed deer are the largest wild animals in Fairfax County. They were nearly extinct at the turn of the 20th century, but careful management has helped them rebound. This deer blends into a large bed of cattail, a native, invasive weed.

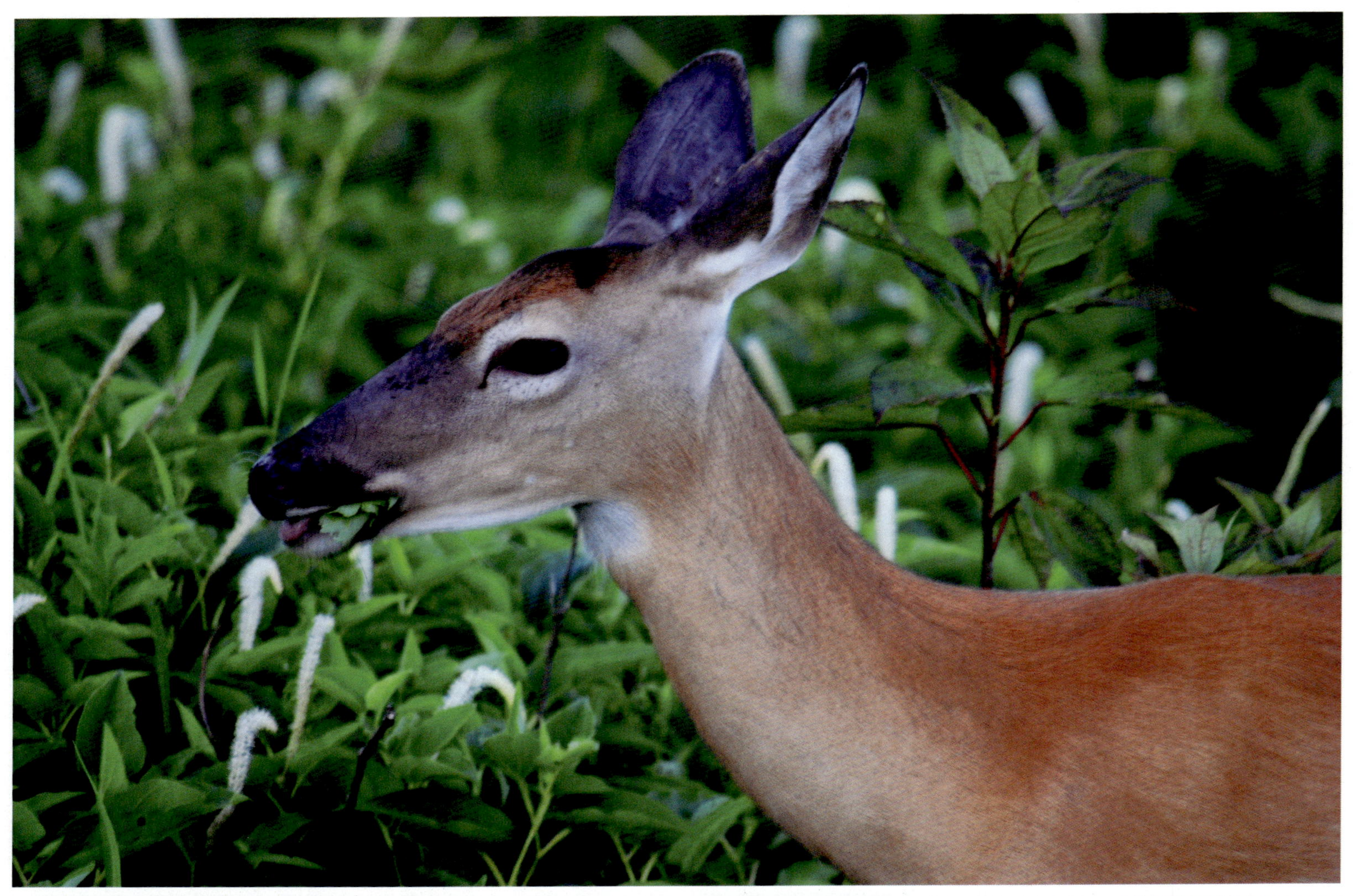

49. A white-tailed deer dines on leaves in the early evening.

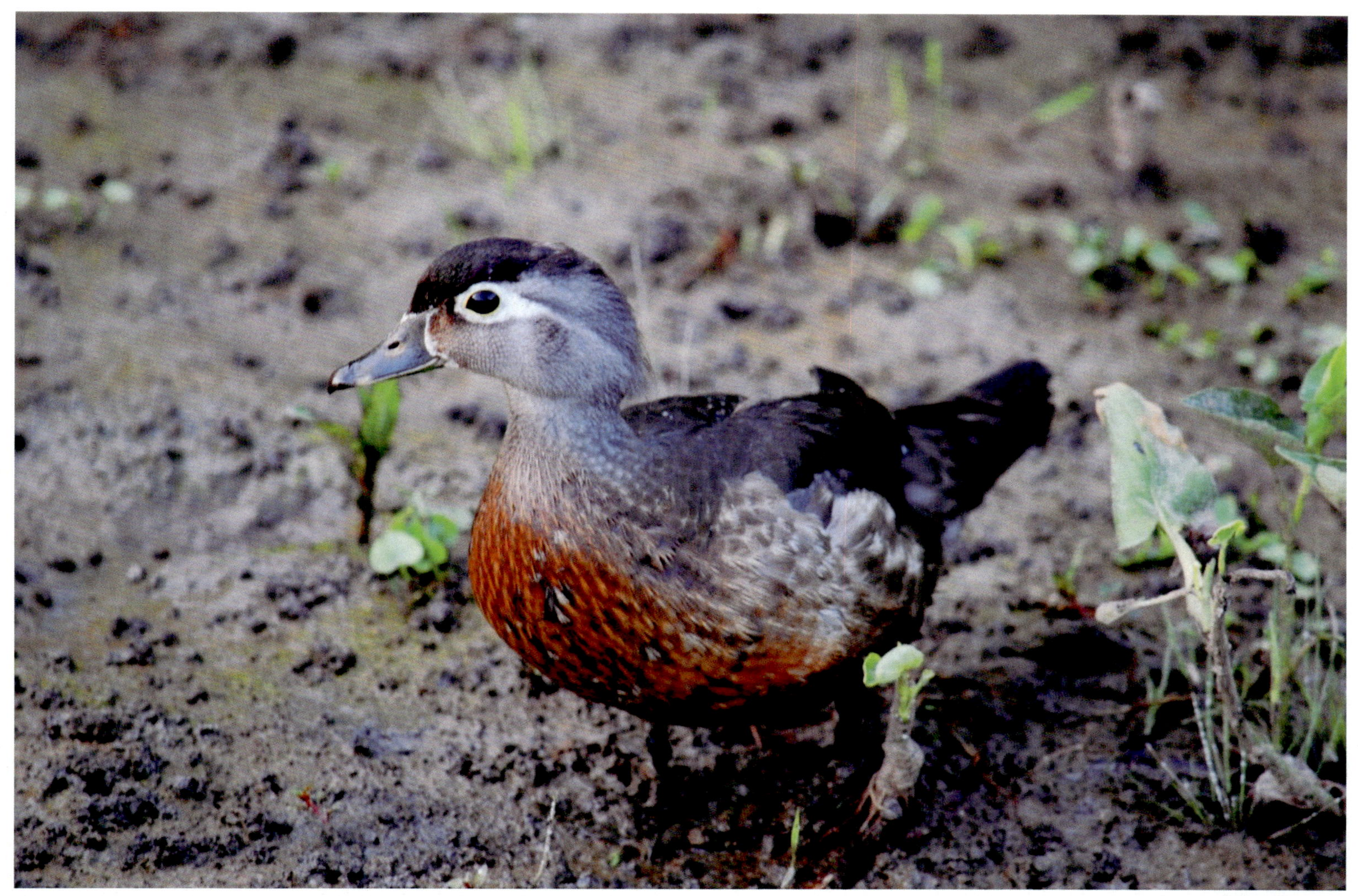

50. Wood ducks like this female are considered among the most beautiful of the waterfowl.

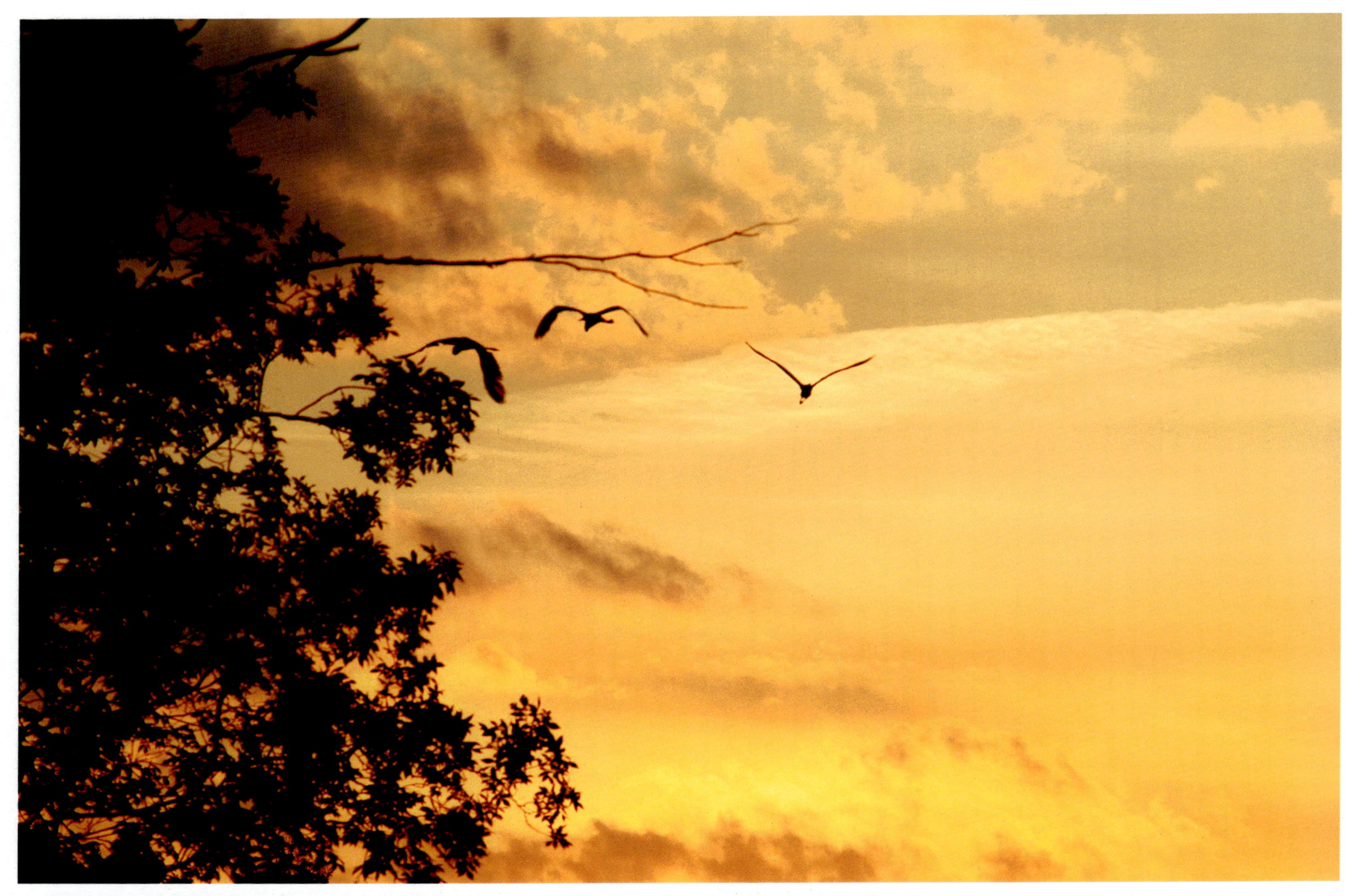

51. Birds move out lethargically on this early evening.

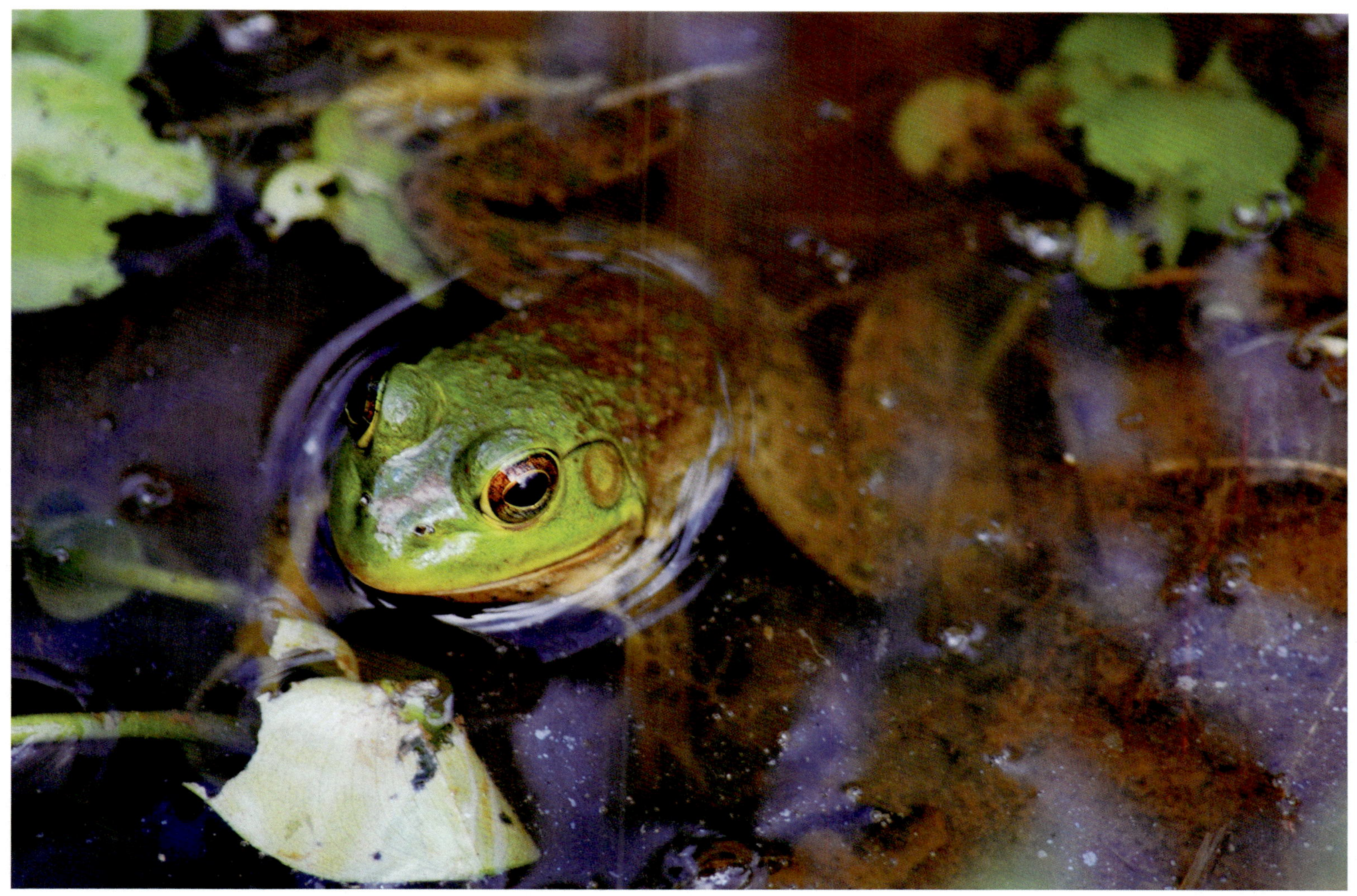

52. Bullfrogs are gifted singers as well as voracious eaters. They will attempt to eat anything that they can fit into their mouths, including birds and snakes.

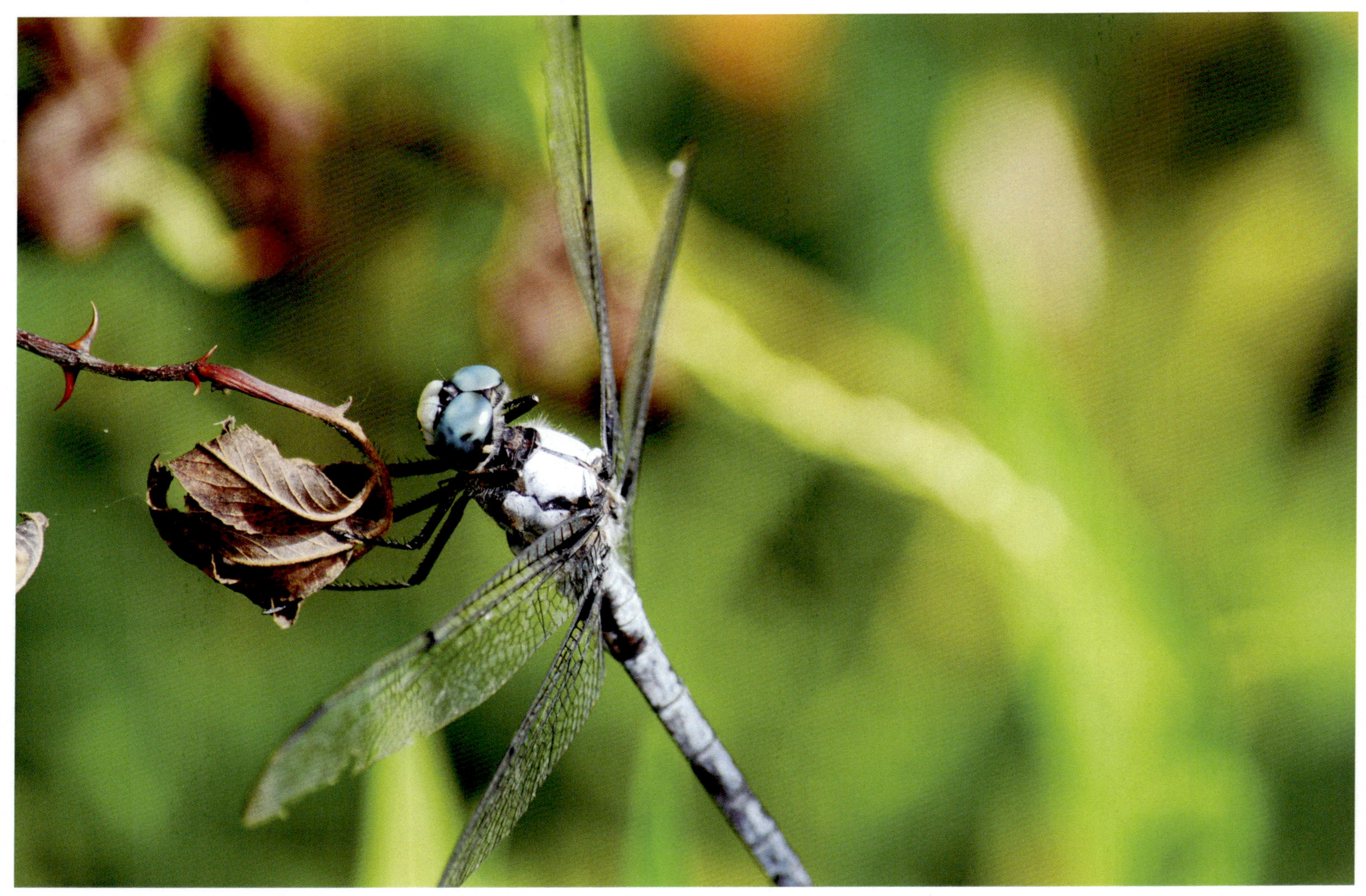

53. The blue skimmer dragonfly has a head that is nearly all eye. It can predict the trajectory of its airborne prey so accurately that it has a near-perfect capture rate.

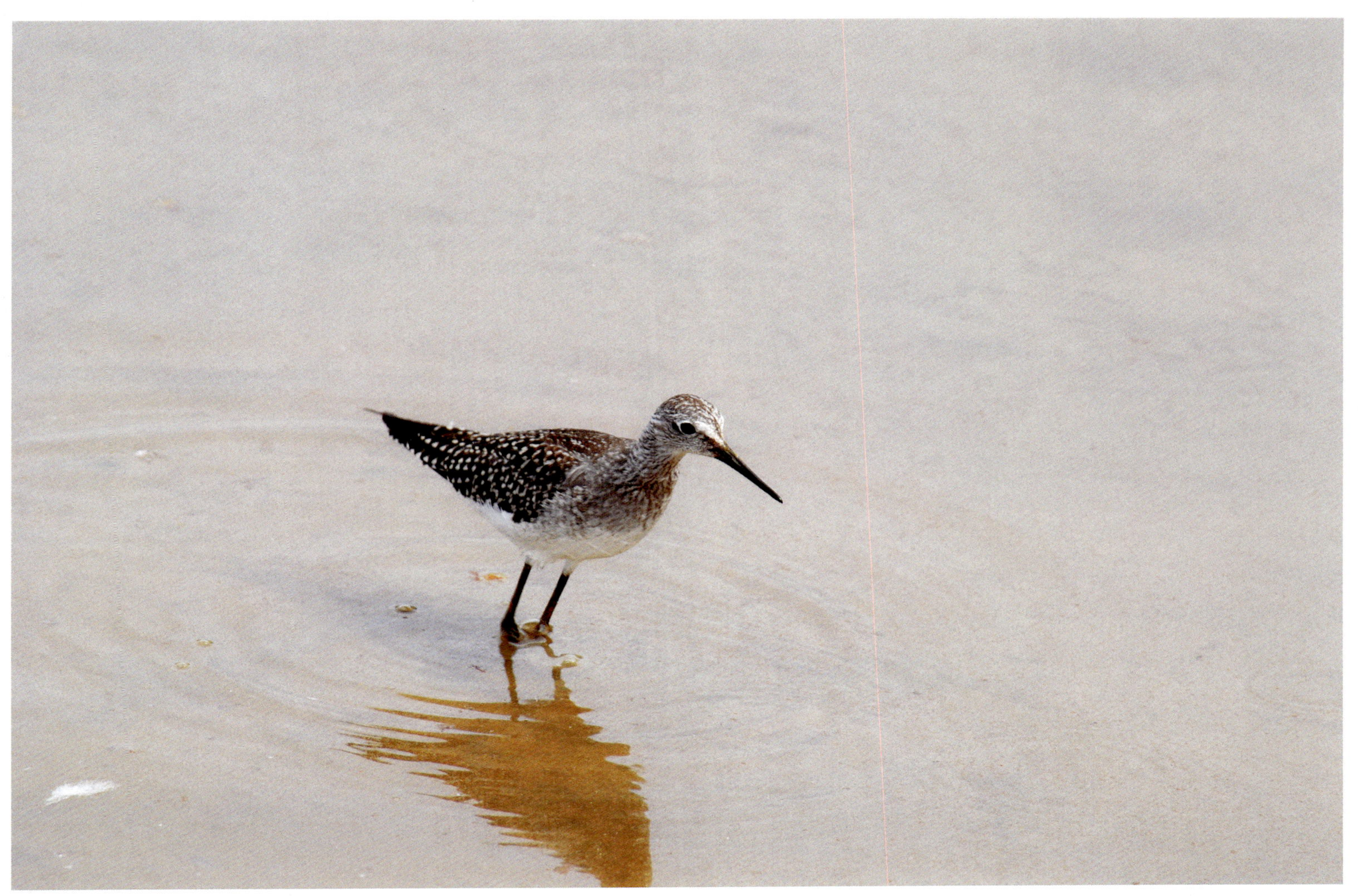

54. This solitary sandpiper is active after an August dry spell that parched some expansive areas of the wetlands.

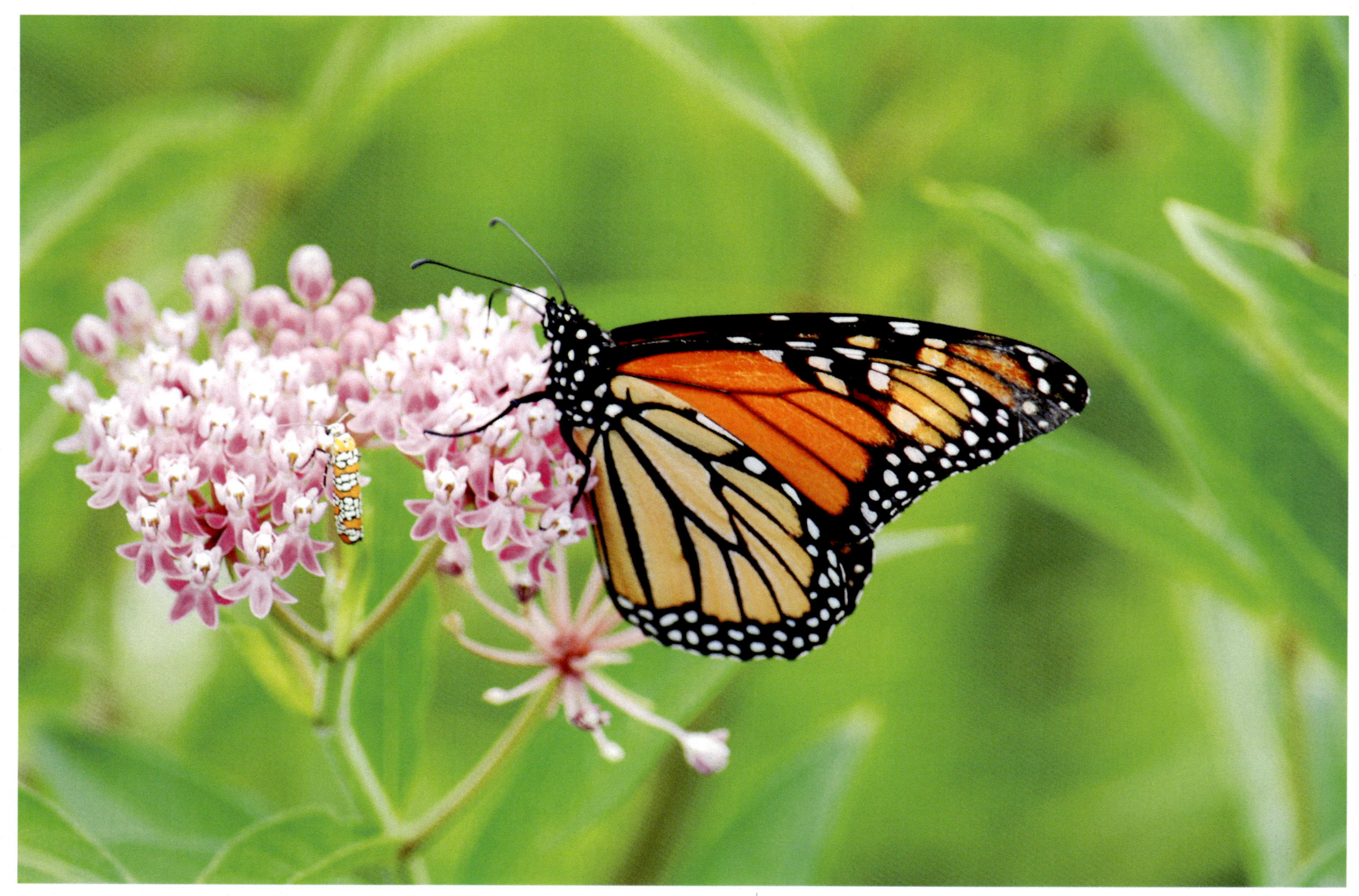

55. The monarch butterfly, known for its winter migrations, thrives on milkweed flowers, a primary source of nutrition for the monarch caterpillar.

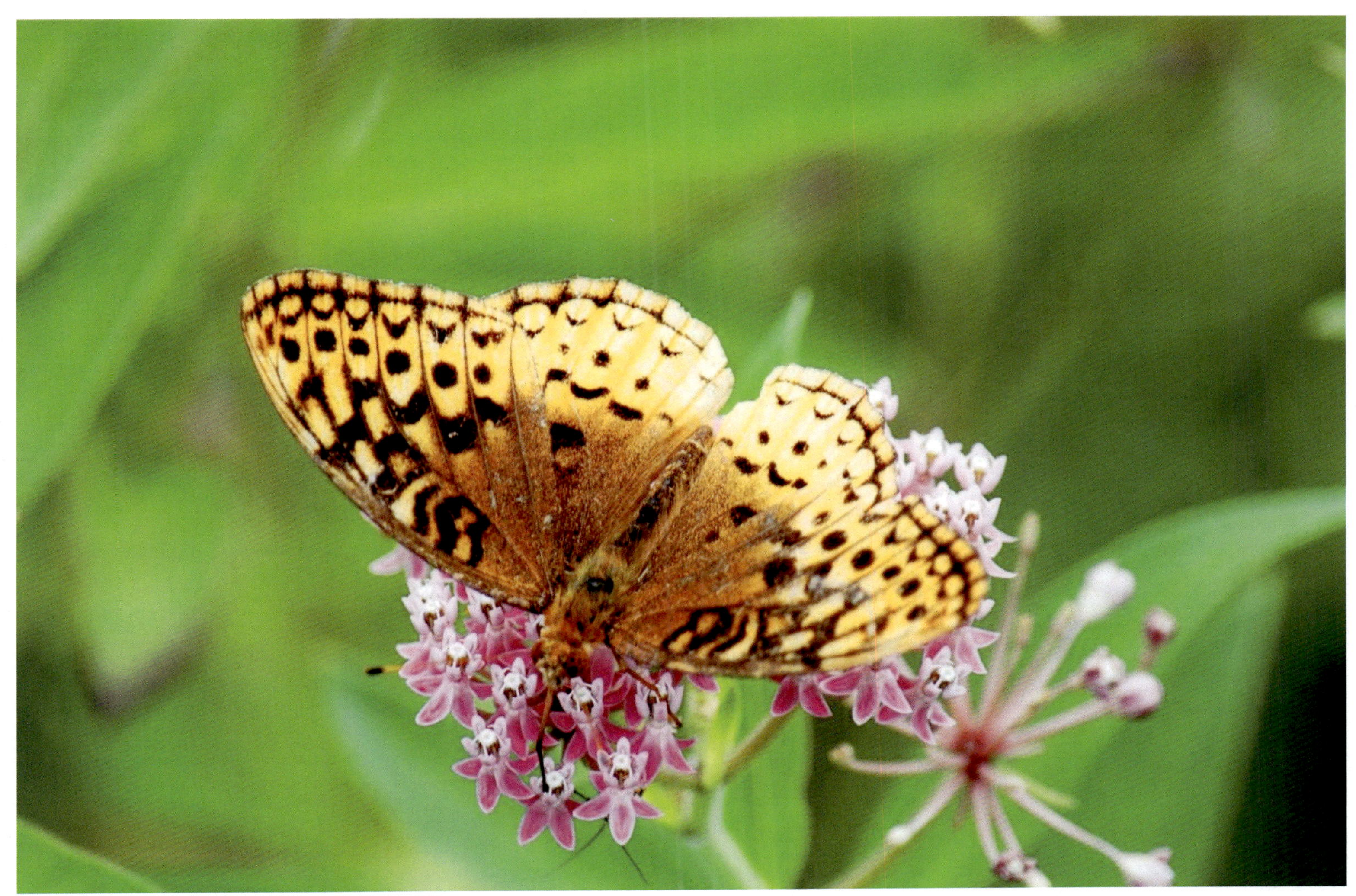

56. The variegated fritillary butterfly with its leopardlike spots adeptly blends into the environment. The female emits pheromones to attract males of its species.

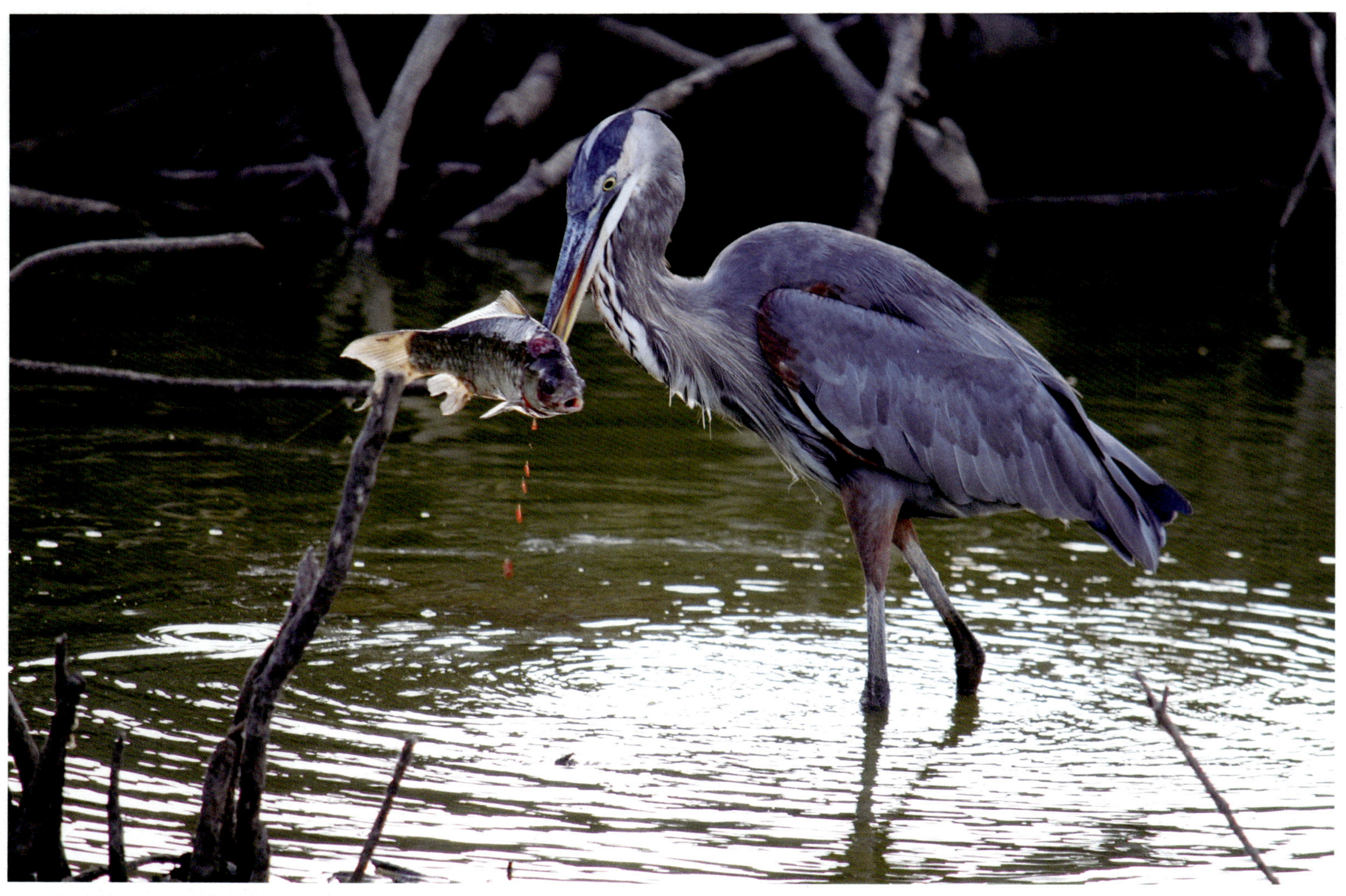

57. The stately, large blue heron can move deceptively slowly when fishing. However, they are lethal to prey with their knife-like bills. This common carp didn't stand a chance.

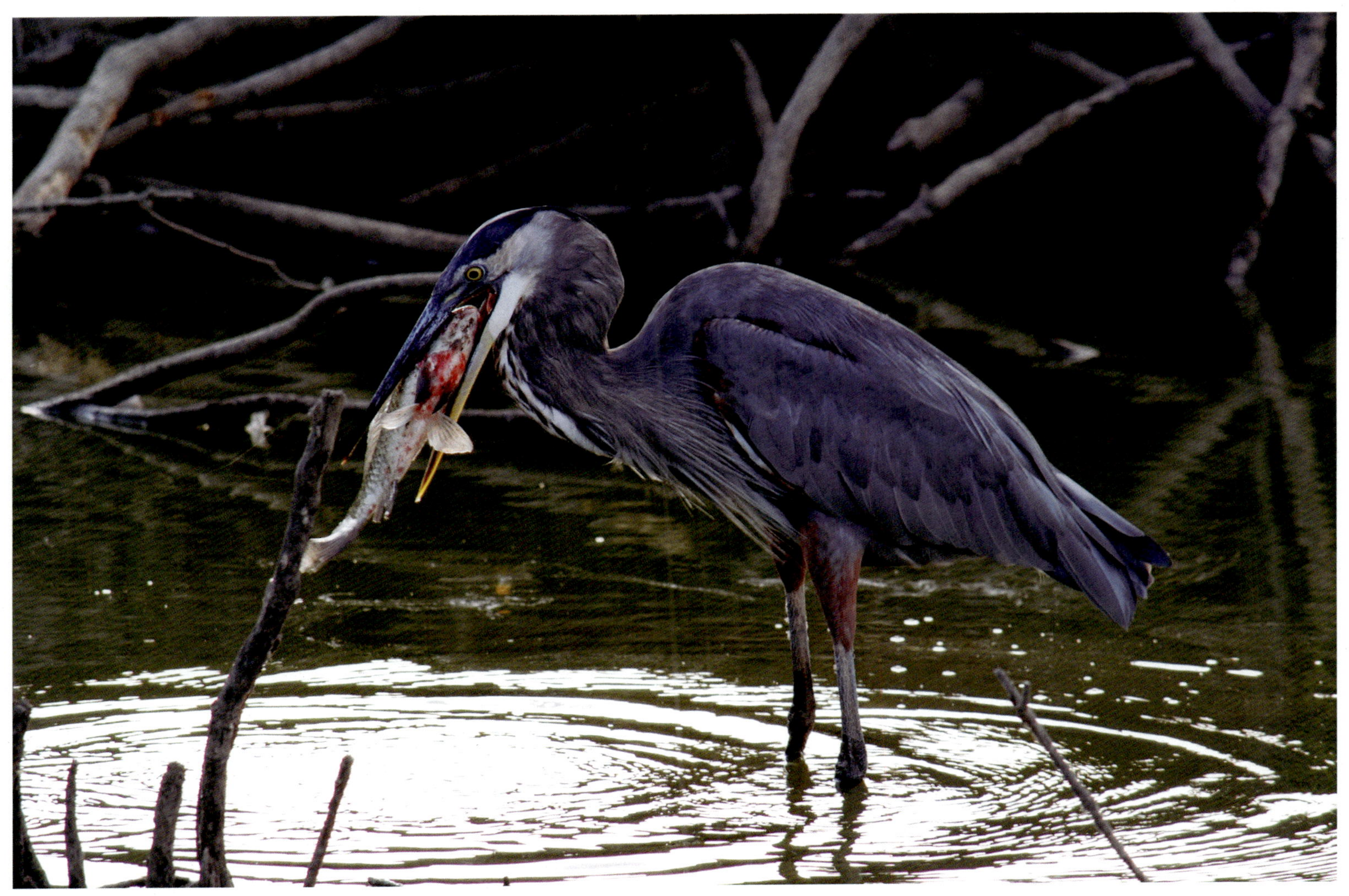

58. Herons can choke on fish when swallowing them whole, but this carp went down fine.

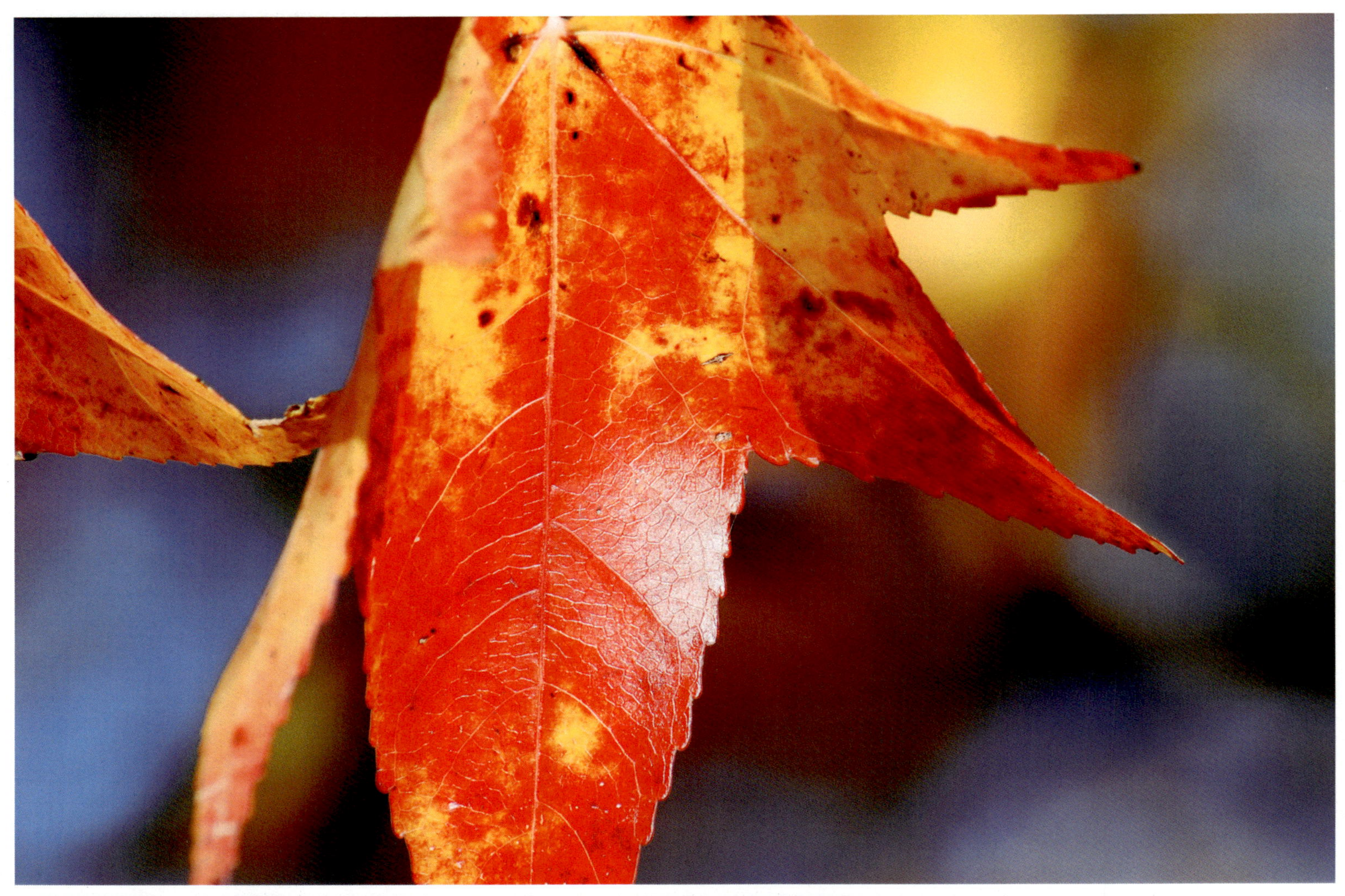

59. The sweetgum tree (liquidambar styraciflua), shown with its fall foliage, can grow to 100 feet.

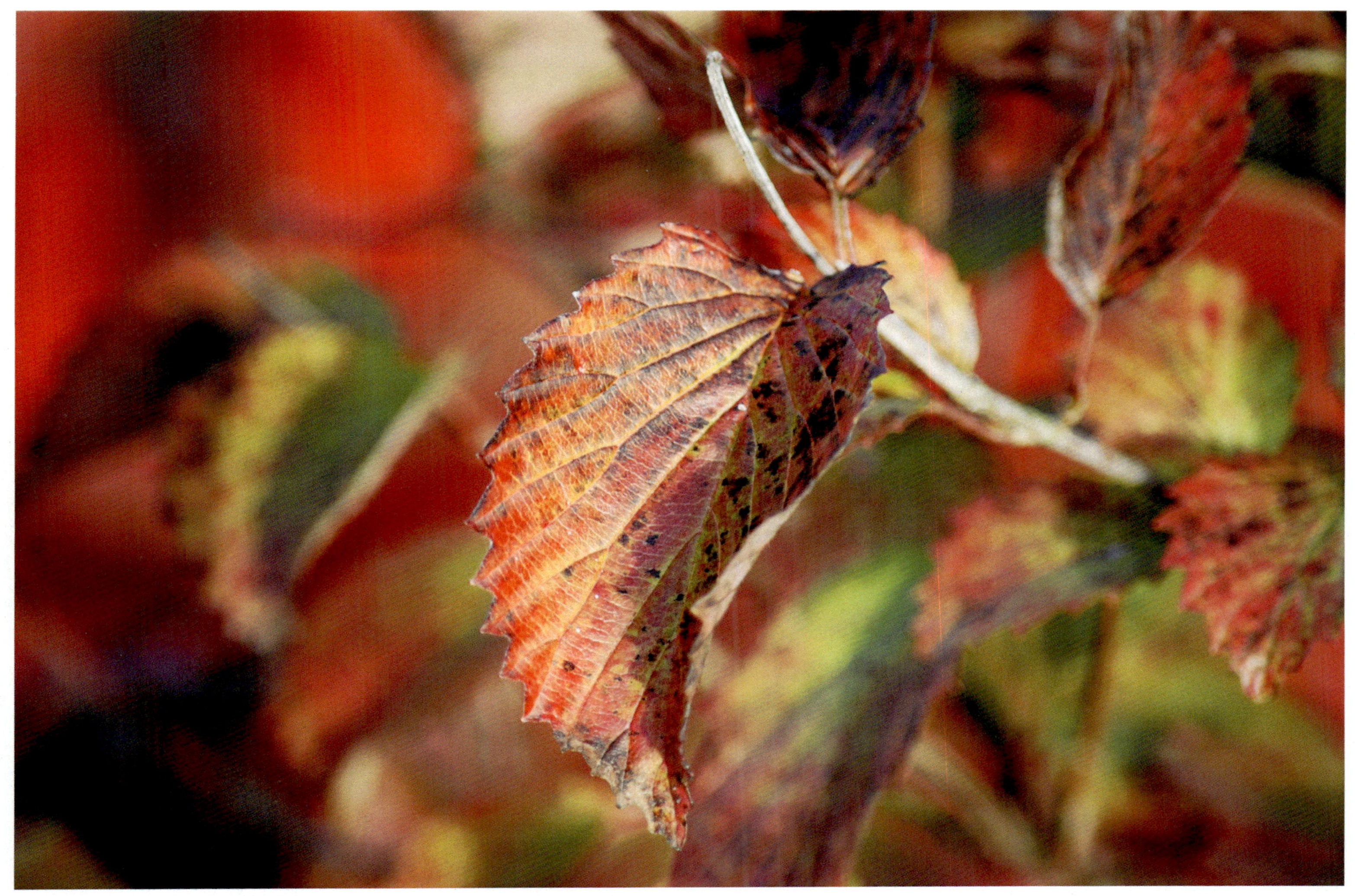

60. The viburnum dentatum, commonly called arrowwood, is a native, multi-stemmed shrub that can grow to nine-feet. Its leaves are in pristine shape as it is free from serious local diseases or insect pests.

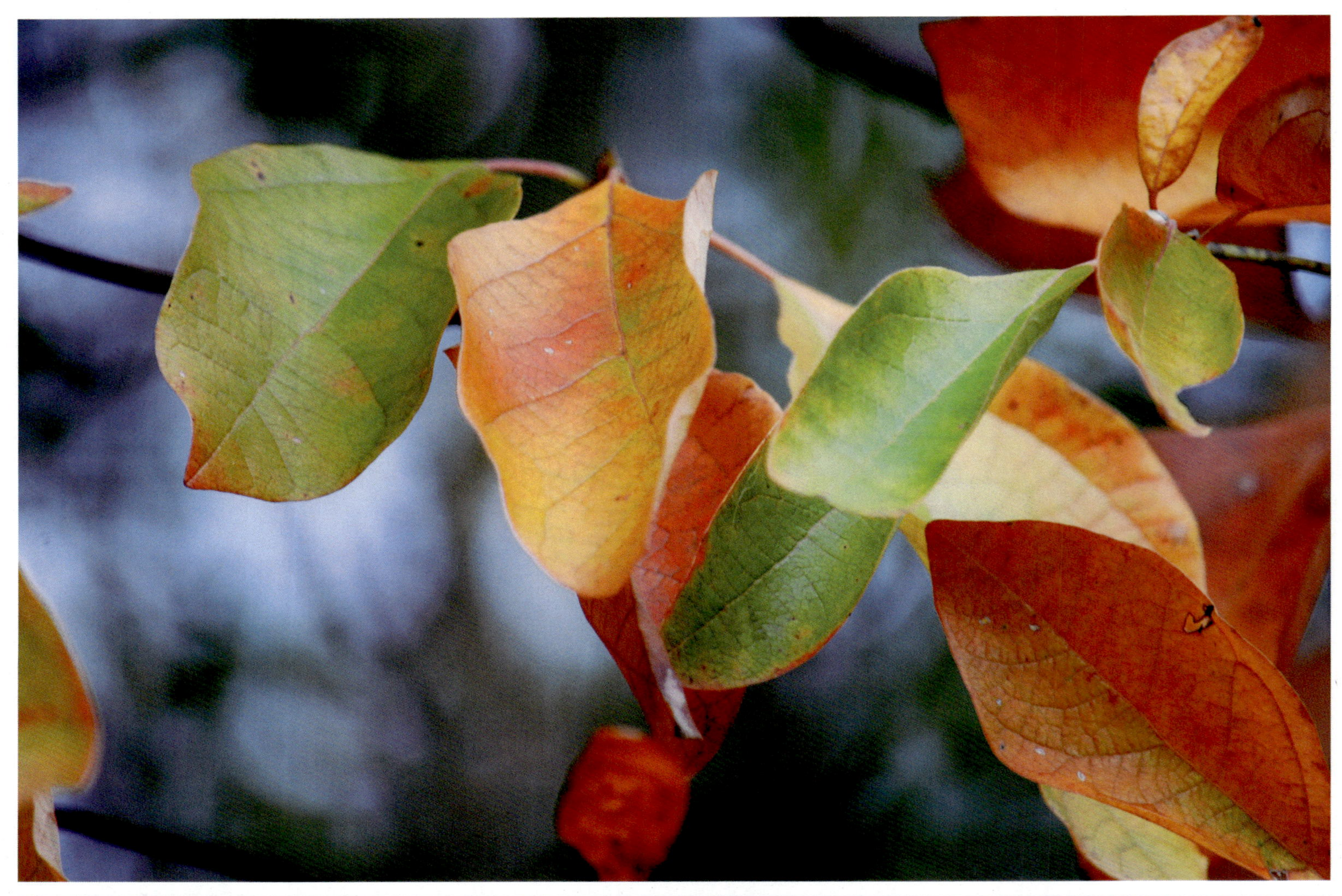

61. The subtly changing fall leaves of the sassafras albidum provide a painter's delight.

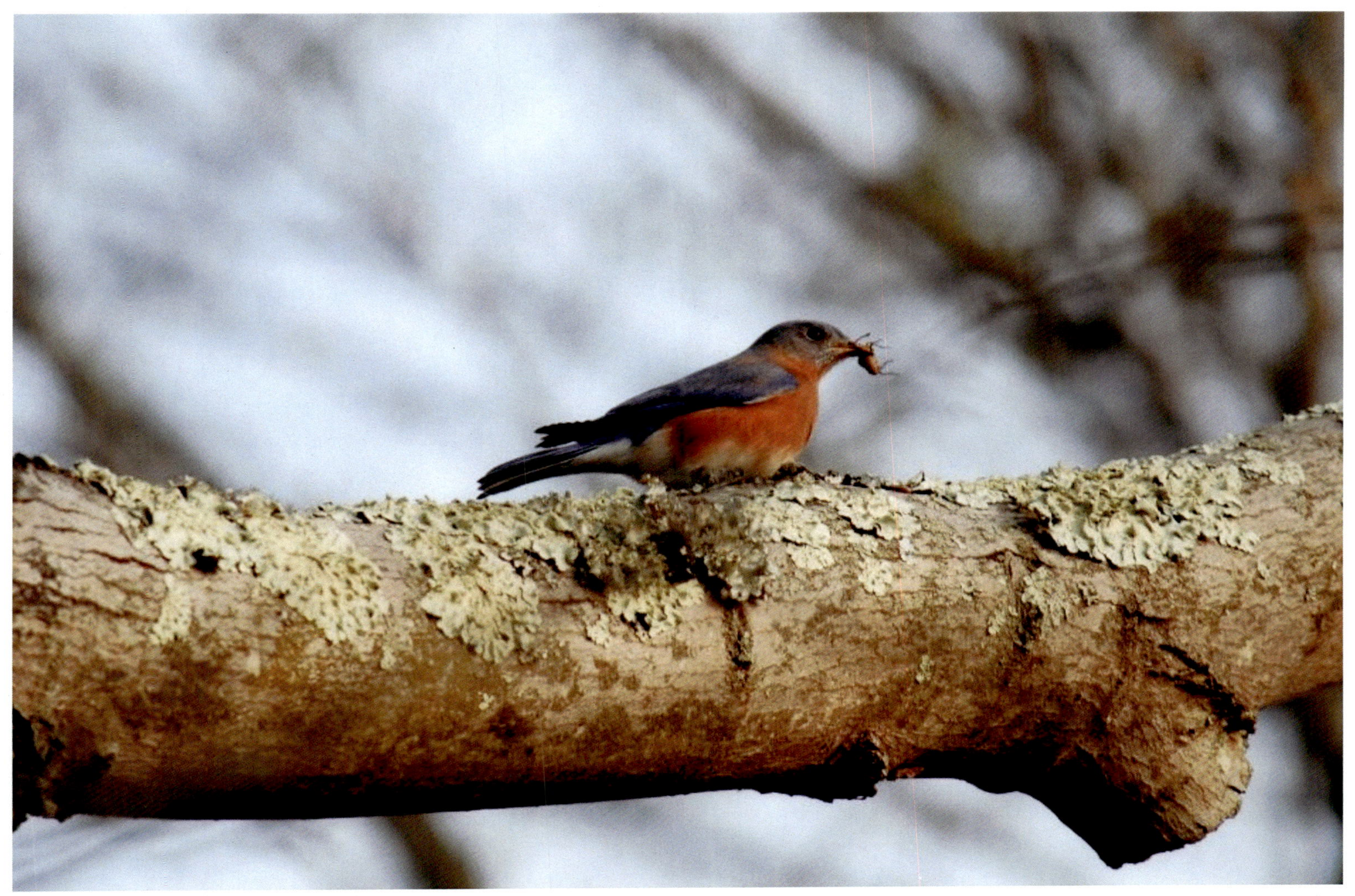

62. The eastern bluebird dines on an insect during an autumn day. These tiny, beautiful birds are enjoying a comeback thanks, in part, to strategically placed, protective nest boxes.

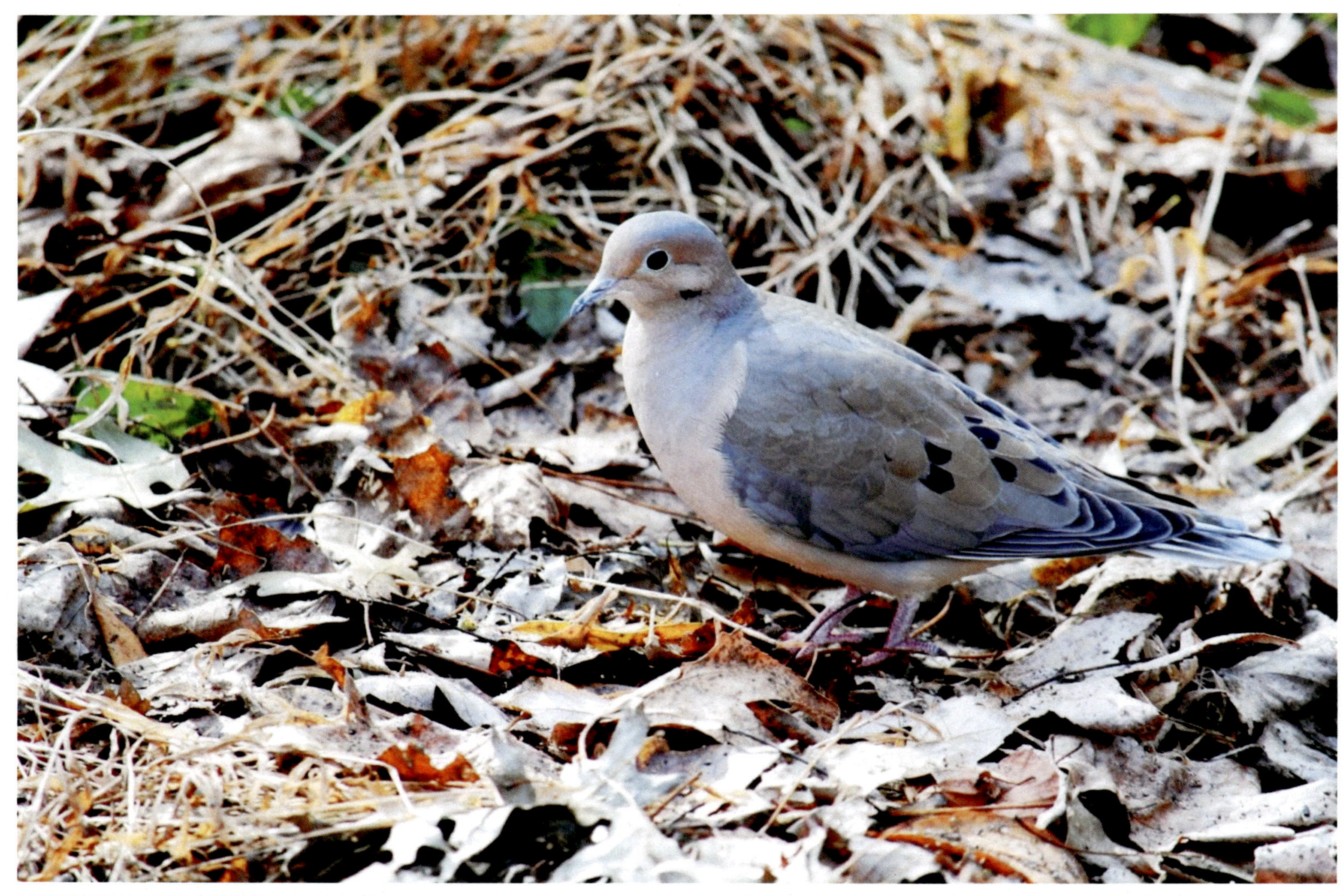

63. The mourning dove is known for its sad songs. It can eat 12-20 percent of its body weight daily, 99 percent of it in seeds.

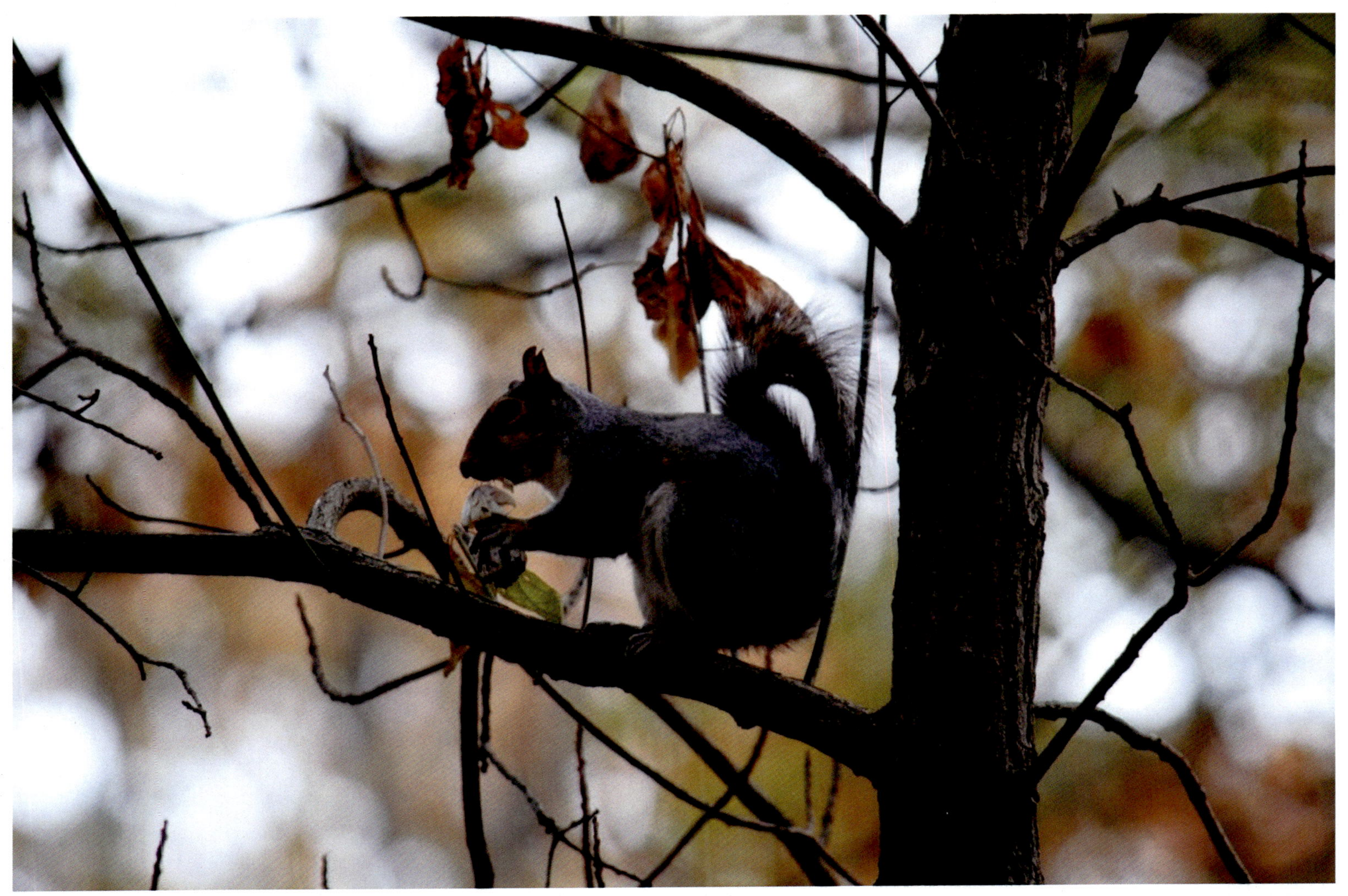

64. An eastern gray squirrel is an abundant species, thriving throughout urban and rural Fairfax County. Since they store more seeds and nuts than they eventually eat, they promote new growth wherever they go.

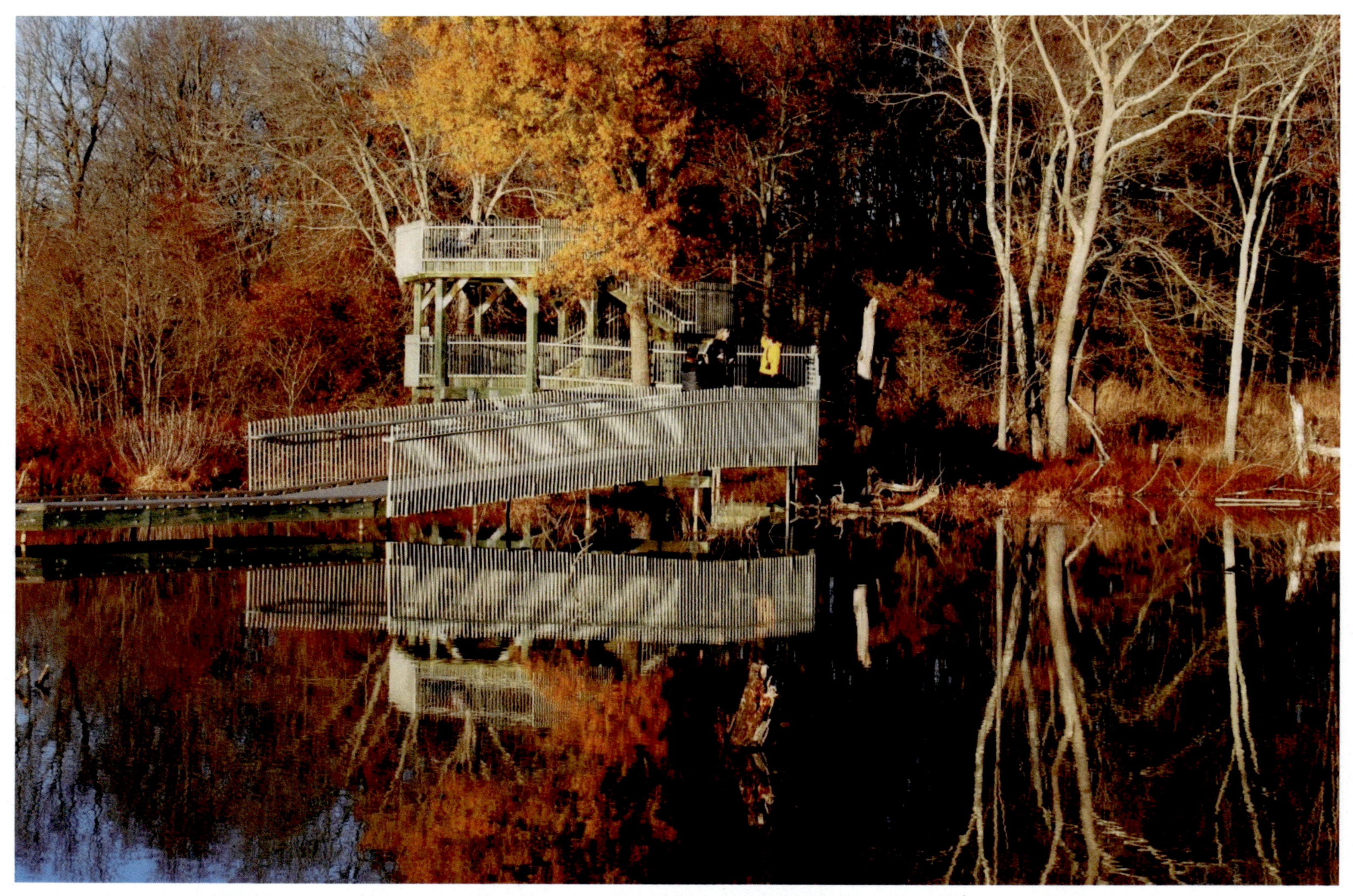

65. The view from the multi-level observation deck is ideal for bird viewing.

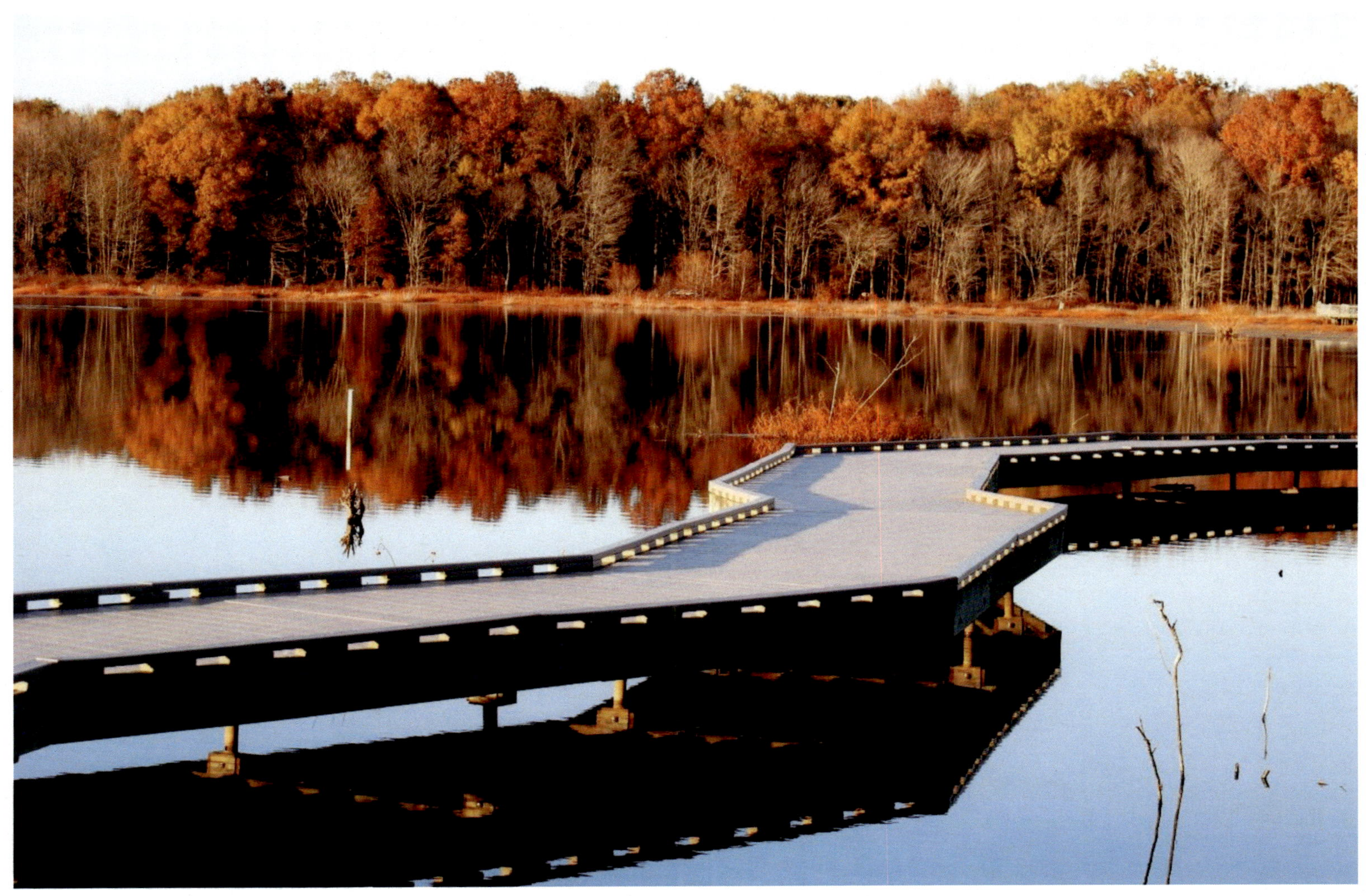

66. Share in one of those moments when the glorious autumnal world simply stops.

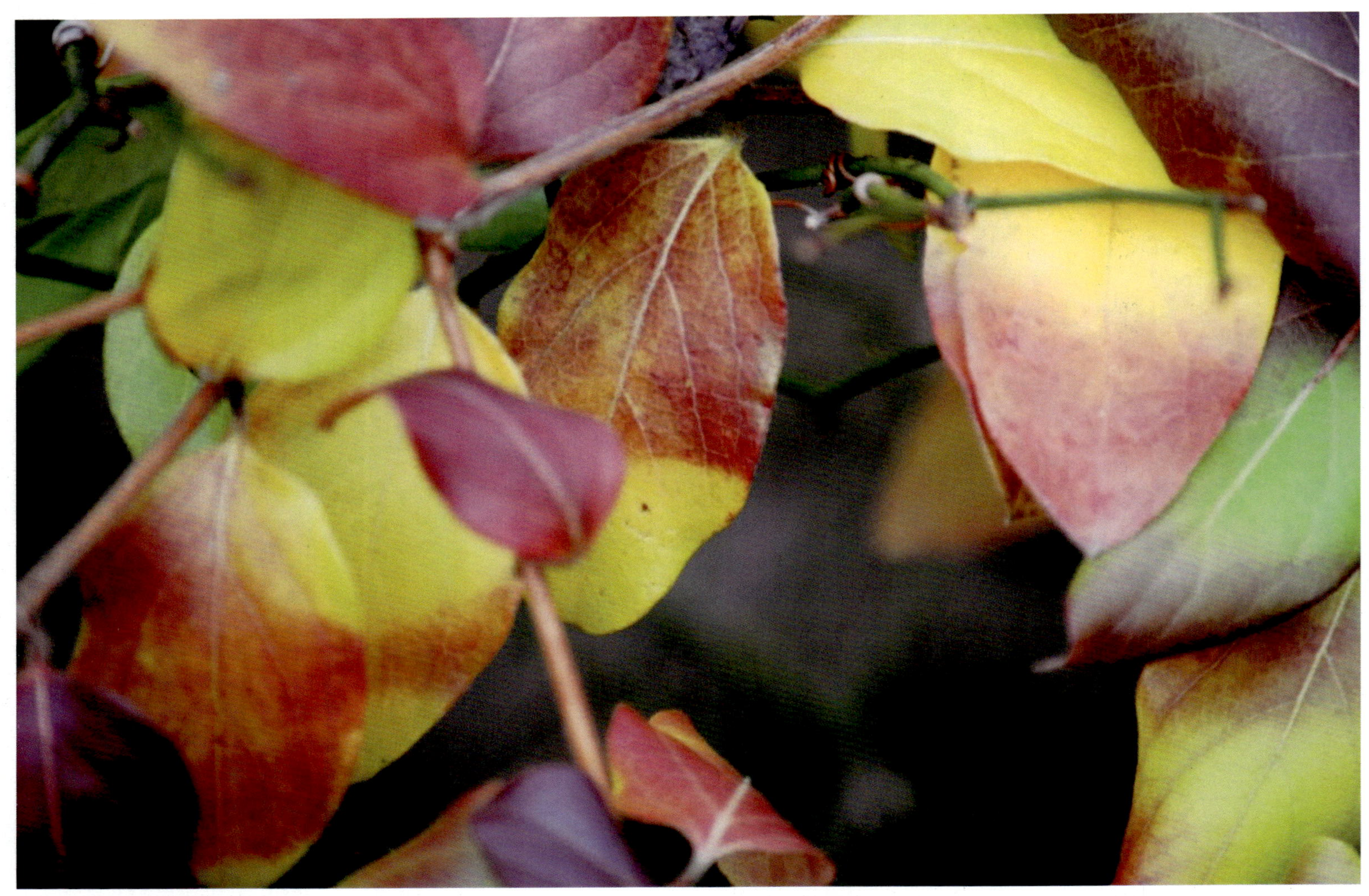

67. The fall leaves of the lonicera japonica, the Japanese honeysuckle, give way to white fragrant spring flowers.

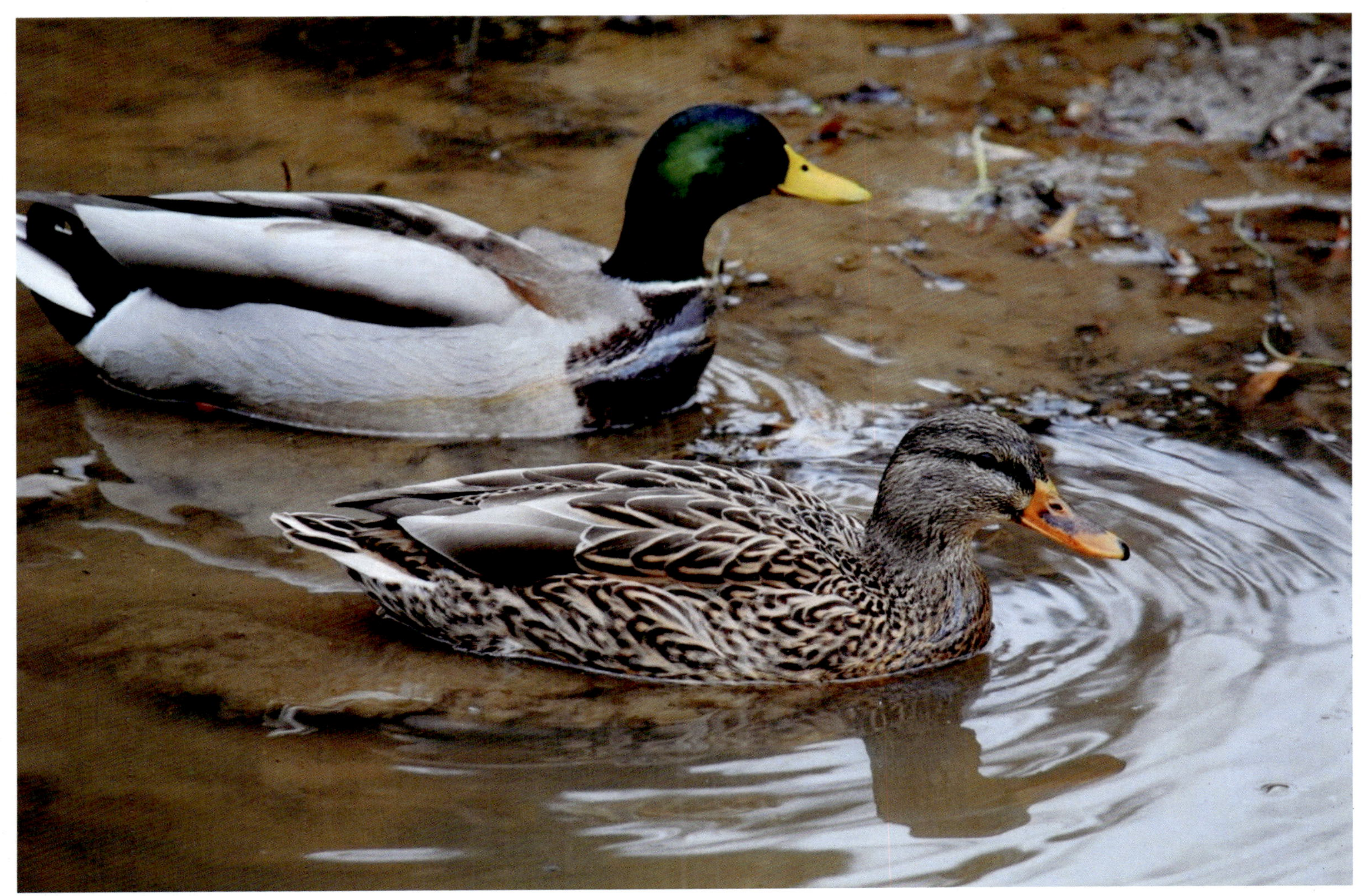

68. Male and female mallards are the most recognizable of large ducks and can fly up to 55 miles per hour.

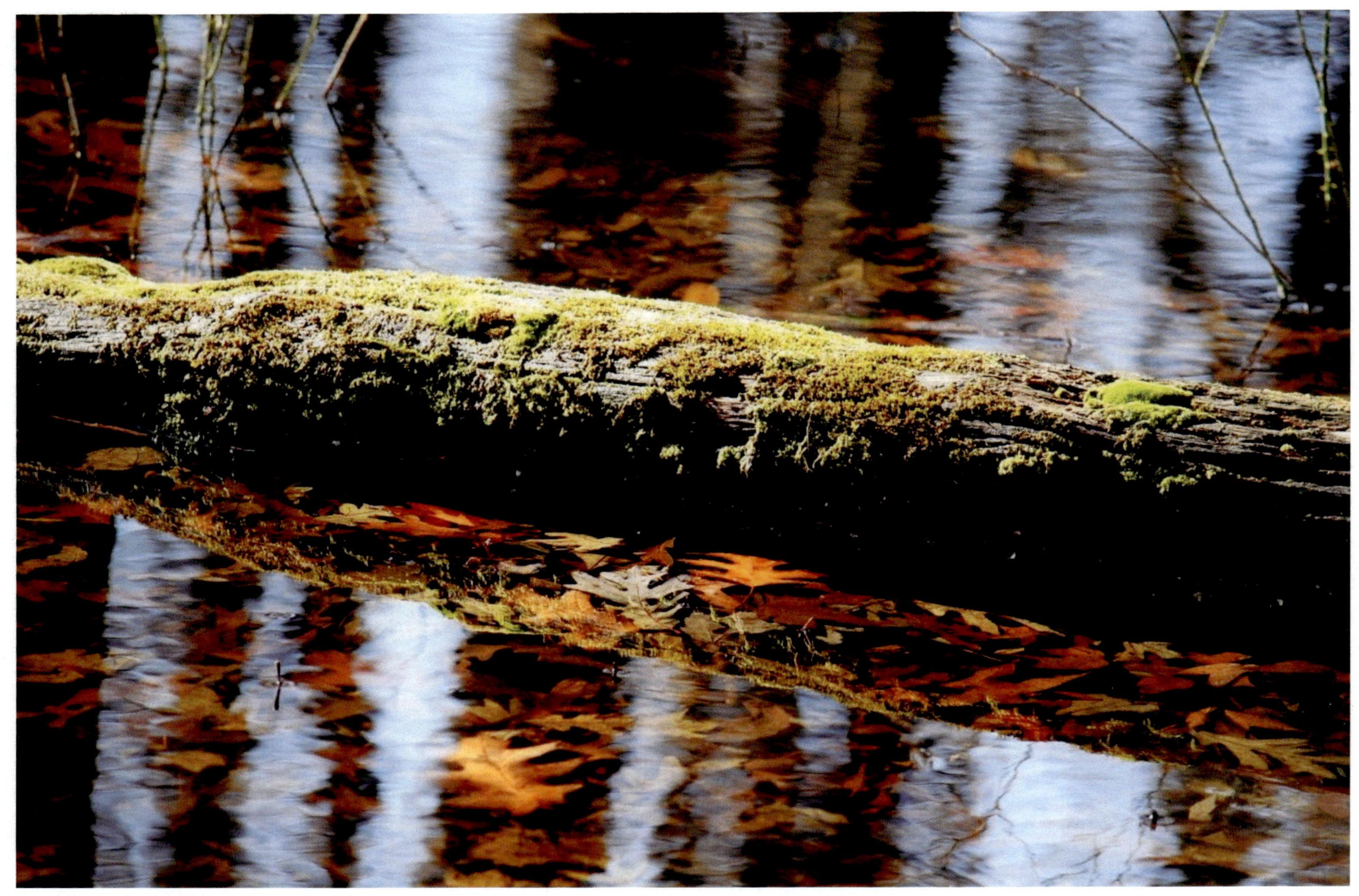

69. Moss in Huntley Meadows is valuable as a shelter for some small insects as well as a food source.

Notes and Bibliography

Chapter 1: Introduction

Introductory quote. Peter D. Moore, scientist and professor, Kings College, London. Wetlands. Chelsea House, 2006. P. XVI.

1. https://www.fairfaxcounty.gov/parks/huntley-meadows/history.

2. http://friendsofhuntleymeadows.org/News%20and%20Events/Newsletter/2014 June/2014_FOHMP_June.pdf.

3. https://www.epa.gov/wetlands/how-do-wetlands-function-and-why-are-they-valuable.

4. https://www.fairfaxcounty.gov/parks/about-us.

5. https://www.mountvernon.org/library/digitalhistory/digital-encyclopedia/article/fairfax-family/

6. https://www.census.gov/quickfacts/fact/table/fairfaxcountyvirginia/PST045218; https://www.bizjournals.com/washington/news/2018/08/28/4-ways-gerald-gordon-built-fairfax-county-into-an.html.

7. https://www.fairfaxcountyeda.org/key-industries/

8. https://www.fairfaxcounty.gov/demographics/fairfax-county-general-overview; https://www.fairfaxcountyeda.org/wp-content/uploads/workforce.pdf; https://www.fairfaxcounty.gov/demographics/fairfax-county-general-overview.

9. https://www.bizjournals.com/washington/news/2017/07/18/greater-washington-has-half-of-the-nations-richest.html.

10. https://nces.ed.gov/fastfacts/display.asp?id=27.

11. https://www.mountvernon.org/

12. https://gunstonhall.org/

13. https://gunstonhall.org/learn/george-mason/virginia-declaration-of-rights/; https://www.archives.gov/founding-docs/virginia-declaration-of-rights.

14. Information courtesy of Fairfax County Chamber of Commerce.

15. Information courtesy of Huntley Meadows; www.friendsofhuntleymeadows.org/News%20and%20Events/
Newsletter/2017/2017_FOHMP_summer.pdf

16. https://vault.sierraclub.org/john_muir_exhibit/writings/steep_trails/chapter_9.aspx.

17. Bosco, Ronald A, Editor. *The Illuminated Walden*. Sterling Publishing, 2002.

Chapter 2: The Virginia Indians

1. Woolley, Benjamin. *Savage Kingdom: The True Story of Jamestown, 1607, and the Settlement of America.*
Harper Collins, 2007. p. 49.

2. Egloff, Keith, and Deborah, Woodward. *First People: The Early Indians of Virginia*. University of Virginia
Press, 2006 by the Virginia Department of Historic Resources; Professor Danielle Moretti-Langholtz, College of William and Mary, provided additional information on estimated population.

3. Humphrey, Robert L., and Mary Elizabeth Chambers, *Ancient Washington: American Indian Cultures of
the Potomac Valley* (Monograph No. 6, Washington, D.C.: Division of Experimental Programs, George
Washington University, 1977).

4. Waldman, Carl. *Atlas of the North American Indian*. 2000, Checkmark Books, NY, NY 10001 Illustrations
by Molly Braun. p.36.

5. https://www.dhr.virginia.gov/first-people-the-early-indians-of-virginia/

6. Huntley Meadows Park: A History. Friends of Huntley Meadows Park.

7. Map of Doeg Creek/Tributary http://www.virginiaplaces.org/graphics/fairfaxwatersheds.jpg; Dogue Run
was one of the farms on George Washington's estate; https://www.mountvernon.org/library/digitalhistory/
digital-encyclopedia/article/dogue-run-farm/

8. Egloff, Keith and Deborah Woodward. *First People: The Early Indians of Virginia*. 2006, University of
Virginia Press by the Virginia Department of Historic Resources. p.17.

9. Ibid. p.17.

10. Welch, Deborah. *Virginia: An Illustrated History*. 2006, Hippocrene Books, New York, New York. P. 24.

11. Captain John Smith, *A Generall Historie of Virginia, New England and the Summer Isles* (Reprint of a 1624 publication, London: I.D. and I.H.for Michael Sparkes, by World Publishing Company, 1966), pp. 22-24, 57-58.

12. Information Courtesy of Professor Danielle Moretti-Langholtz, College of William and Mary.

Chapter 3: The Nineteenth Century — Historic Huntley Manor

1. https://www.fairfaxcounty.gov/parks/historic-huntley.

2. Brown, Charlotte. *Groveton. Images of America* series. 2013, Arcadia Publishing, Charleston, South Carolina. pp. 9-10; https://gunstonhall.org/learn/george-mason/

3. Wren, Tony P. *A Mason Family Country House*, 1971.Published by the Fairfax County Division of Planning under the direction of the County Board of Supervisors in cooperation with the County History Commission. Fairfax Virginia. Project Gutenberg. p. 41.

4. Schwartz, Steven A. "Forgotten Father." May 2000, *Smithsonian Magazine*; Information provided by Historic Gunston Hall; http://www.connectionnewspapers.com/news/2002/aug/06/george-mason-and-family-legacy-of-liberty/ August 6, 2002. p.1

5. Moxham, Robert Morgan. *The Colonial Plantations of George Mason*. Colonial Press, North Springfield, Virginia, 1975. p.1.

6. https://founders.archives.gov/

7. https://www.mountvernon.org/preservation/maps/extent-of-washingtons-1793-mount-vernon-land-holdings/

8. https://www.fairfaxcounty.gov/parks/historic-huntley.

9. Roberts, William J. *Lost Alexandria. An Illustrated History of Sixteen Destroyed Historic Homes in and Around Alexandria, Virginia.* 2017, Voyage Publishing, Alexandria, Virginia. P.16.

10. Ibid. p.16.

11. https://www.fairfaxcounty.gov/parks/historic-huntley/;http://www.historichuntley.org/Huntleys_History.html.

12. http://www.historichuntley.org/Newsletter_files/FOHH-News-0313.pdf.

13. Mauro, Charles V. *The Civil War in Fairfax County*. The History Press, 2006. p.80.

14. https://www.fairfaxcounty.gov/parks/historic-huntley/

15. Brown, Charlotte. *Groveton*. *Images of America* series. 2013, Arcadia Publishing, Charleston, South Carolina. p. 10

16. https://www.fairfaxcounty.gov/parks/historic-huntley/

17. https://www.fairfaxcounty.gov/planning-development/historic/national-register.

Chapter 4: The Twentieth Century —
The George Washington Air Junction (1929-1937)

1. https://www.faa.gov/about/history/brief_history/

2. https://history.nasa.gov/SP-09-511.pdf.

3. https://www.flyreagan.com/dca/history-reagan-national-airport.

4. *Free Lance Star-Fredericksburg*. February 9, 1929; "Capital is Offered Grounds for Great Airport in Virginia," *Washington Post*. December 11, 1928.

5. "Man's Triumph in the Air is Near." *The Atlanta Constitution;* July 27, 1919.

6. https://www.newspapers.com/clip/5782652/el_paso_herald/; https://www.history.com/news/aviation-con-man-henry-woodhouse January 11, 2019.

7. "Capital is Offered Grounds for Great Airport in Virginia," *Washington Post,* December 11, 1928. "World's Greatest Air Center," *Alexandria Gazette*, Northern Virginia Industrial Edition. January 1, 1930.

8. "Huge Flying School Planned in Virginia," *Washington Post*. May 16, 1929.

9. https://www.fairfaxcounty.gov/circuit/sites/circuit/files/assets/documents/pdf/hrc/fita/fita-september-2019.pdf.

10. https://www.britannica.com/technology/zeppelin; https://www.newspapers.com/clip/5777292/the_indianapolis_news/ Hybla Valley may be chosen as a base for ocean liners. 11 July 1930, p. 14; *Dress and Vanity Fair*, 1913. Henry Woodhouse, *Across the Atlantic Through the Air*.

"R-101 (Blimp) in Second Test Today." *New York Times*. October 18, 1929.

11. Friends of Huntley Meadows Park. June, 2015.

12. "Air Junction Site Formally Opened. Dedication of Field Named for George Washington Attracts Notables," February 23, 1929. *Washington Post*.

13. www.friendsofhuntleymeadows.org/News%20and%20Events/Newsletter/2015/2015_FOHMP_June.pdf.

14. Ibid. *Aviation Week* July 6, 1929.

15. https://www.history.com/news/aviation-con-man-henry-woodhouse.

16. https://www.americanheritage.com/ignoble-profession.

17. Ibid.

Chapter 5: The Era of U.S. Government Use —
The Bureau of Public Roads (1944-1954)

1. https://www.fairfaxcounty.gov/parks/huntley-meadows/history.

2. Federal Highway Administration, United States Department of Transportation. Information courtesy of Richard Weingroff, Federal Highway Administration Historian.

3. America's Highways, 1776 to 1976. Federal Highway Administration Report, 1976.

4. http://onlinepubs.trb.org/Onlinepubs/hrbbulletin/168/168-001.pdf.

5. https://archive.org/details/annualreportbure1951unit/page/n55.

6. https://archive.org/details/annualreportbure1951unit/page/n45.

7. www.virginiadot.org/about/resources/historyofrds.pdf (p. 30).

8. Ibid. p. 34.

9. www.virginiadot.org/about/resources/historyofrds.pdf (p. 35).

10. www.virginiadot.org/about/resources/historyofrds.pdf (p. 36).

11. www.virginiadot.org/about/resources/historyofrds.pdf (p. 37).

12. https://www.census.gov/prod/2002pubs/censr-4.pdf (p. 32).

13. https://www.census.gov/prod/2002pubs/censr-4.pdf. (p. 11).

14. https://www.fairfaxcountyeda.org/history-fairfax-county-virginia.

15. *Washington Post,* May 27, 1956. Hybla Valley field to be used for Army, Navy Tests.

Chapter 6: The Cold War Years —
The National Guard Anti-aircraft Station (1951-1957)

1. Friends of Huntley Meadows: A History.

2. https://www.history.com/topics/cold-war/cold-war-history and https://history.state.gov/departmenthistory/short-history/worldin1945.

3. https://history.state.gov/milestones/1945-1952/foreword.

4. Historical background provided by Diplomatic Historian Christopher Bright; https://nationalsecurity.gmu.edu/christopher-bright/; https://apps.dtic.mil/dtic/tr/fulltext/u2/a339158.pdf%20antiaircraft%20and%20postwar%20history. p. 1, 1995, Colonel Steven Moller. "Vigilant and Invincible," *Air Defense Military Magazine*; http://www.connectionnewspapers.com/news/2016/may/12/missiles-and-guns-backyard-and-school-parking-lot/

5. Huntley Meadows Park: A History.

6. Historical background provided by Diplomatic Historian Christopher Bright. https://nationalsecurity.gmu. edu/christopher-bright.

7. *Rings of Supersonic Steel. Air Defenses of the United States Army*, 2002. Mark Morgan and Mark A. Berhow.

Chapter 7: The Age of Space Satellites — Naval Research Laboratory (1957-1971)

1. Huntley Meadows: A History. Friends of Huntley Meadows.

2. Evolution of Naval Radio-Electronics. Contributions of the Naval Research Laboratory, Louis A. Gebhard, 1979. NRL Report 8300. P. 407-409. https://apps.dtic.mil/dtic/tr/fulltext/u2/a084225.pdf.

3. U.S. Navy/NRO Program C Electronic Intelligence Satellites (1958-1977) Declassified Report, Ronald L. Potts. p.5. https://www.nro.gov/Portals/65/documents/foia/docs/U.S.%20Navy-NRO%20Program %20C%20 Electronic%20Intelligence%20Satellites%20(1958-1977).pdf.

4. Evolution of Naval Radio-Electronics. Contributions of the Naval Research Laboratory, Louis A. Gebhard, 1979. NRL Report 8300.p.iii https://apps.dtic.mil/dtic/tr/fulltext/u2/a084225.pdf.

5. "Wide Aperture Direction-Finder with Sleeve Antennas." Raymond F. Gleason and Robert M. Greene. 20 August 1958. Declassified Naval Research laboratory document. Report Number 843. p.1 https://apps.dtic. mil/dtic/tr/fulltext/u2/a459666.pdf.

6. Ibid. p. 2

7. https://www.pbs.org/wgbh/nova/article/sputnik-impact-on-america/

8. Information provided by Angelina Callahan, Ph.D., Naval Research Laboratory Historian.

9. https://www.nrl.navy.mil/accomplishments/rockets/vanguard-project/

10. Wide Aperture Direction-Finder With Sleeve Antennas Raymond F. Gleason and Robert M. Greene. 20 August 1958. Declassified Naval Research Laboratory document. Report Number 843. P.2 https://apps.dtic. mil/dtic/tr/fulltext/u2/a459666.pdf.

11. https://www.fairfaxcounty.gov/parks/huntley-meadows/history.

Note: As described by the National Park Service, the process of declaring a parcel of federal property surplus includes offering it through the federal General Services Administration (GSA) to other agencies in case they are interested.

Chapter 8: The Federal Legacy of Parks Program

1. https://www.fordlibrarymuseum.gov/library/document/0126/1489951.pdf.

2. Ibid.

3. https://www.nixonfoundation.org/2010/06/legacy-of-parks/

4. Ibid.

5. https://www.nps.gov/orgs/1508/index.htm; Information courtesy of Wendy Ormont, Program Leader, Federal Land to Parks Program, National Park Service.

6. https://www.nps.gov/subjects/lwcf/congressionalacts.htm.

7. https://www.nps.gov/subjects/lwcf/upload/Public-Law-91-485.pdf.

8. Information courtesy of Karen Sheffield, Manager, Huntley Meadows park.

9. https://www.fordlibrarymuseum.gov/library/document/0126/1489951.pdf.

10. Invitation to Huntley Meadows Park dedication. Courtesy of Fairfax County Library.

11. Information courtesy of Karen Sheffield, Manager, Huntley Meadows Park.

12. Information courtesy of Wendy Ormont, Program Leader, Federal Land to Parks Program, National Park Service.

13. Ibid.

Chapter 9: The Boardwalk Restoration (2011)

1. https://www.washingtonian.com/2015/05/04/huntley-meadows/ May 4, 2015.

2. http://www.friendsofhuntleymeadows.org/News%20and%20Events/Newsletter/2015/2015_FOHMP_September.pdf.

3. www.friendsofhuntleymeadows.org/News%20and%20Events/Newsletter/2015/2015_FOHMP_June.pdf. 3. https://www.fairfaxcounty.gov/parks/huntley-meadows/history.

4. Ibid. http://friendsofhuntleymeadows.org/News%20and%20Events/Newsletter/2011/December%202011/FOHMP%20Dec%202011.pdf.

5. https://fairfaxnews.com/2011/06/huntley-meadows-boardwalk-to-close-for-repairs/

6. http://www.tmgworld.net/portfolio-item/huntley-meadows-park-boardwalk-renovation/#

7. Ibid.

8. https://www.atsdr.cdc.gov/sites/KerrMcGee/docs/Creosote%20Health%20Effects%20(Tronox).pdf.

9. https://www.fairfaxcounty.gov/parks/huntley-meadows/history.

10. www.tmgworld.net/portfolio-item/huntley-meadows-park-boardwalk-renovation/#

Chapter 10: The Wetlands Restoration (2013-2014)

1. https://www.fairfaxcounty.gov/parks/sites/parks/files/assets/documents/nature-history/huntleymeadows/celebrating-fifth-anniversary-huntley-meadows-wetland-restoration%20(002).pdf.

2. Ibid.

3. https://www.fairfaxcounty.gov/parks/huntley-meadows/wetland-restoration; www.huntleymeadows.org/wetland_restoration.html.

4. http://www.washingtonpost.com/wp-dyn/content/article/2009/01/19/AR2009011902642.html?
noredirect=on%20January%2025,%202009. A hemi-marsh is a type of wetland typically found in deeper
water. Hemi-marshes have a mix of emergent vegetation and submersed plant life. This combination creates
an ideal habitat for a variety of aquatic-dependent birds and amphibians Migrating birds find this place ideal
for stopping over and many brooding female birds find this a perfect place for raising young. https://www.
fairfaxcounty.gov/parks/huntley-meadows/wetland-restoration

5. https://www.fairfaxcounty.gov/parks/huntley-meadows/wetland-restoration.

6. Information Courtesy of Wetland Studies Solutions.

7. https://www.nationalgeographic.com/animals/mammals/b/beaver/

8. http://www.washingtonpost.com/wp-dyn/content/article/2009/01/19/AR2009011902642.html?
noredirect=on%20January%2025,%202009; https://www.savingwetlands.com/wetland-restoration/huntley-
meadows-park-wetlands-restoration-project/; https://alextimes.com/2007/08/wetlands-restoration-plan-in-
store-for-huntley-mea/.

9. https://www.wetlands.com/huntley-meadows-wetland-restoration.

10. Information Courtesy of Wetland Studies Solutions.

11. Wetland Studies and Solutions, *Restoring A Natural Resource Treasure in Northern Virginia*. The Central
Wetland Area of Huntley Meadows Park. Wetland Studies and Solutions report, September/October, 2015;
https://wtop.com/news/2013/04/bulldozers-to-invade-va-park-full-of-beavers-snakeheads/slide/1/

12. http://www.connectionnewspapers.com/news/2014/jul/17/commentary-celebrating-huntley-meadows-
wetland-res/

13. https://vnps.org/conservation/virginia-native-plant-registry-sites-3/huntley-meadows/ b.http://www.huntley
meadows.org/HMdocuments/Huntley%20Meadows%20Research%20Report%20Final%204-15-15.pdf.

14. Information Courtesy of Wetland Studies Solutions.

15. Restoring A Natural Resource Treasure in Northern Virginia. The Central Wetland Area of Huntley
Meadows Park. Wetland Studies and Solutions report, September/October, 2015.

16. https://www.deq.virginia.gov/Portals/0/DEQ/PollutionPrevention/GEEA/2017GEEAProgram.pdf
f?ver=2017-04-03-163416-223.

17. http://www.connectionnewspapers.com/news/2014/jul/17/commentary-celebrating-huntley-meadows-wetland-res/friendsofhuntleymeadows.org/News%20and%20Events/Newsletter/2019/2019_FOHMP_spring_08k.pdf; https://vnps.org/virginia-native-plant-registry-sites/huntley-meadows/

Chapter 11: The Value of Our Wetlands

1. https://www.nationalgeographic.org/encyclopedia/wetland/ https://www.usgs.gov/faqs/why-are-wetlands-important.

2. https://nepis.epa.gov/Exe/ZyPDF.cgi/200053Q1.PDF?Dockey=200053Q1.pdf.

3. https://www.epa.gov/wetlands/how-do-wetlands-function-and-why-are-they-valuable;

   https://www.wetlandswork.org/wetland-benefits.

4. http://www.huntleymeadows.org/wetland_restoration.html.

5. https://www.fairfaxcounty.gov/parks/huntley-meadows/wetland-restoration.

6. https://www.aswm.org/wetlands/about-wetlands.

7. www.dof.virginia.gov/water/wetland-values.htm; https://defenders.org/wild-places/wetlands-and-rivers.

8. https://www.fws.gov/wetlands.

9. https://unfccc.int/news/wetlands-disappearing-three-times-faster-than-forests.

Chapter 12: The Value of Our Forests

1. http://www.dof.virginia.gov/infopubs/_forest-facts/FF-Why-We-Need-Trees_pub.pdf.

2. https://www.americanforests.org/issues/climate/

3. https://www.fs.fed.us/learn/trees.

4. https://www.arborday.org/trees/treefacts/

5. Ibid.

6. https://www.fs.fed.us/openspace/fote/reports/nrs-62_sustaining_americas_urban.pdf.

7. https://wwf.panda.org/our_work/forests/importance_forests/

8. https://www.fs.fed.us/openspace/fote/reports/nrs-62_sustaining_americas_urban.pdf.

9. Friends of Huntley Meadows, Winter 2020.

10. Smithsonian Migratory Bird Center, National Zoologic Park.

Chapter 13: The Legacy of Norma Hoffman

1. www.connectionnewspapers.com/news/2017/jun/26/remembering-norma-hoffman/

2. https://www.legacy.com/obituaries/washingtonpost/obituary.aspx?pid=185817875.

3. http://www.connectionnewspapers.com/news/2013/jun/13/recogniton-norma-hoffmans-commitment-environmental/

4. https://www.pariscityvision.com/en/paris-by-night/moulin-rouge/cabaret-history.

5. https://www.southbeachmagazine.com/latin-quarter-nightclub/

6. https://www2.census.gov/library/publications/decennial/1940/population-volume-1/33973538v1ch05.pdf p. 84.

7. https://loc.gov/teachers/classroommaterials/presentationsandactivities/presentations/timeline/depwwii/art/

8. http://www.connectionnewspapers.com/news/2017/jun/26/remembering-norma-hoffman/

9. http://www.connectionnewspapers.com/news/2013/jun/13/recogniton-norma-hoffmans-commitment-environmental/

10. https://www.nytimes.com/1984/11/08/us/pentagon-spokesman-gets-reporter-as-aide.html.

11. http://www.connectionnewspapers.com/news/2013/jun/13/recogniton-norma-hoffmans-commitment-environmental/

12. Friends of Huntley Meadows newsletter. Summer, 2017.

13. Ibid. p. 8.

14. http://www.friendsofhuntleymeadows.org/News%20and%20Events/Newsletter/2006/FOHM.PApr2006NL.pdf.

15. http://connectionarchives.com/PDF/2010/090810/Mt%20Vernon.pdf. Huntley Meadows Rescued by Community. September 9, 2010.

16. "Fairfax Alters Road Plan in Bid to Aid Wetlands: Lockheed-Van Dorn Project report issued," *Washington Post*. July 15, 1987; http://www.friendsofhuntleymeadows.org/News%20and%20Events/Newsletter/2006/FOHMPApr2006NL.pdf.

17. "$135 Bond on Fairfax Ballot," *Washington Post*. November 3, 1985.

18. "United States Park Service Approves Highway," *Washington Post*. July 20, 1983.

19. "Springfield Bypass Still on Drawing Board," *Washington Post*. April 18, 1987.

20. "Residents Upset Over Park Road: Huntley Meadows Impact Questioned," *Washington Post*, May 23, 1985.

21. http://connectionarchives.com/PDF/2010/090810/Mt%20Vernon.pdf. Huntley Meadows Rescued by Community. September 9, 2010; http://www.friendsofhuntleymeadows.org/News%20and%20Events/Newsletter/2006/FOHMPApr2006NL.pdf.

22. Ibid.

23. "Three U.S. Agencies Oppose Van Dorn Street Extension," *Washington Post*. January 12, 1995. "Fairfax Won't Build Controversial Road in Wetlands Park," *Washington Post*. December 4, 1990.

24. http://www.friendsofhuntleymeadows.org/Norma.html.

25.   Ibid.

26.   http://www.connectionarchives.com/PDF/2010/020310/Mt%20Vernon.pdf; https://patch.com/virginia/greateralexandria/photos-historic-huntley-prepares-for-grand-opening.

27.   Booth, Glenda, C. Zebra Press. June, 2019. p. 38. www.historichuntley.org/Friends_of_Historic_Huntley.html.

28.   http://www.historichuntley.org/Special_Huntley_Tours.html.

29.   https://www.fairfaxcounty.gov/parks/huntley-meadows/visitor-center.

30.   Information courtesy of Fred Hoffman.

31.   https://www.fairfaxcounty.gov/parks/huntley-meadows/visitor-center.

32.   http://www.connectionnewspapers.com/news/2017/jun/26/remembering-norma-hoffman/

33.   Background information provided by Lisa Hoffman.

Bibliography

American Forests Organization, "Restoring America's Forest Landscapes." https://www.americanforests.org/issues/climate/ Accessed September 2019.

Arbor Day Foundation, "Tree Facts." https://www.arborday.org/trees/treefacts/ Accessed September 2019.

Association of State Wetland Managers, "About Wetlands." https://www.aswm.org/wetlands/about-wetlands. Accessed September 2019.

Booth, Glenda, C. *Historic Huntley Mansion: Mysteries Still Abound, Waiting to be Unraveled*, Zebra Press. June 2019. p. 38. digital.thezebra.org/?issueID=38&pageID=38

Bosco, Ronald A, Editor. *The Illuminated Walden*. New York, Sterling Publishing Company, 2002. p.10.

Bright, Christopher. Diplomatic Historian, George Mason University. Provided defense-related documents and maps. Conversations occurred from February to October 2019.

Brown, Charlotte. *Groveton. Images of America Series*. 2013. Charleston, South Carolina: Arcadia Publishing, pp. 9,10.

Brown, Joseph. "The Latin Quarter Nightclub," *South Beach Magazine*. May 16, 2004. https://www.southbeach magazine.com/latin-quarter-nightclub/.

Byron, Jim. "Legacy of Parks," June 14, 2010. Richard Nixon Foundation. https://www.nixonfoundation. org/2010/06/legacy-of-parks/. Accessed July, 2019.

Dickson, Paul, "Sputnik's Impact on America. Public Broadcasting Service (PBS)," November 6, 2007. https://www.pbs.org/wgbh/nova/article/sputnik-impact-on-america/

Egloff, Keith, and Deborah Woodward, *First People: The Early Indians of Virginia*. University of Virginia Press, the Virginia Department of Historic Resources. 2006. p.5.

Federal Aviation Administration. "A Brief History of the FAA." https://www.faa.gov/about/history/brief_history/ Accessed March, 2019.

Gebhard, Louis A. *Evolution of Naval Radio-Electronics. Contributions of the Naval Research Laboratory*, 1979. NRL Report 8300. pp. 407-409.

Gilgore, Sara. "Greater Washington Has Half of the Nation's Richest Counties," July 18, 2017. *Business Journals, The*. https://www.bizjournals.com/washington/news/2017/07/18/greater-washington-has-half-of-the-nations-richest.html

Gleason, Raymond F. and Robert M. Greene, "Wide Aperture Direction-Finder with Sleeve Antennas." August 20, 1958. Declassified Naval Research Laboratory document. Report Number 843. p.1. https://apps.dtic.mil/dtic/tr/fulltext/u2/a459666.pdf

Gunston Hall. "Historic Gunston Hall." https://gunstonhall.org/ Accessed June, 2019.

Humphrey, Robert L., and Mary Elizabeth Chambers. *Ancient Washington: American Indian Cultures of the Potomac Valley* (Monograph No. 6) 1977. Washington, D.C.: Division of Experimental Programs, George Washington University.

Jeffers, Robinson. *Not Man Apart*. Sierra Club Press, San Francisco, 1969. p. 4.

Keats, John. *The Complete Poems*. Penguin Classics, London. 1977. p. 106.

Lengel, Edward G. "An Ignoble Profession," *American Heritage Magazine*. Fall, 2011, Volume 61, Issue 2.

Mauro, Charles V. *The Civil War in Fairfax County*. 2006. Charleston, South Carolina: The History Press. p.80.

Moeller, Steven, Colonel, "Vigilant and Invincible," *Air Defense Artillery Military*. 1995, https://apps.dtic.mil/dtic/tr/fulltext/u2/a339158.pdf%20antiaircraft%20and%20postwar%20history. p.1.

Moore, Peter D. *Wetlands: Biomes of the Earth*. 2006. New York, N.Y: Infobase Publishing. p. XVI.

Moore, Peter D. https://epdf.tips/wetlands-biomes-of-the-earth.html

Moretti-Langholtz, Danielle, Professor. College of William and Mary. Conversations in July 2019.

Morgan, Mark, and Mark A. Berhow, *Rings of Supersonic Steel. Air Defenses of the United States Army*, 2002. Bodega Bay, California: Hole in the Head Press. pp 1-7.

Mount Vernon Organization, "George Washington's Mount Vernon." https://www.mountvernon.org/ Accessed June, 2019.

Moxham, Robert Morgan. *The Colonial Plantations of George Mason.* 1975. North Springfield, Virginia: Colonial Press. p.1.

National Center on Education Statistics. "Educational Attainment," https://nces.ed.gov/fastfacts/display.asp?id=27. Accessed November, 2018.

Ormont, Wendy. Program Leader, National Park Service. Conversations from May 2019 to February 2020.

Oxford University. *Oxford Book of Quotations.* 1980. Oxford University.

Potts, Ronald, L. *U.S. Navy/NRO Program C Electronic Intelligence Satellites (1958-1977)* Declassified Report. p. 5.

Reagan National Airport. "History of Regan National Airport." https://www.flyreagan.com/dca/history-reagan-national-airport. Accessed November, 2018.

Roberts, William Jay. *Lost Alexandria. An Illustrated History of Sixteen Destroyed Historic Homes in and Around Alexandria, Virginia.* 2017. Alexandria, Virginia: Voyage Publishing, p.16.

Schwartz, Steven A. "Forgotten Father." May, 2000, *Smithsonian Magazine.* Reprinted by *Mason Spirit Magazine* Fall, 2001. George Mason University. pp.7-9.

Sheffield, Karen. Manager, Huntley Meadows Park. Conversations from 2018-2020.

Sierra Club. John Muir Exhibit. "Mormon Lilies." https://vault.sierraclub.org/john_muir_exhibit/writings/steep_trails/chapter_9.aspx. Accessed October, 2018.

Silverberg, Hank. "Bulldozers to invade Va. Park Full of Beavers, Snakeheads." April 2, 2013. https://wtop.com/news/2013/04/bulldozers-to-invade-va-park-full-of-beavers-snakeheads/slide/1/

Smith, John (Captain). *A Generall Historie of Virginia, New England and the Summer Isles* (Reprint of a 1624 publication, London: I.D. and I.H.for Michael Sparkes, World Publishing Company, 1966), pp. 22-24, 57-58.

Sugarman, Joe. "Why Huntley Meadows is the Best Park for Kids. *Washingtonian Magazine*. May 4, 2015. Volume 50, Number 8. https://www.washingtonian.com/2015/05/04/huntley-meadows/
TMG Construction. "Huntley Meadows Park Boardwalk Renovation." www.tmgworld.net/portfolio-item/ huntley-meadows-park-boardwalk-renovation/#. Accessed June 2019.

U.S. Census. "Quick Facts, Fairfax County, Virginia." https://www.census.gov/quickfacts/fact/table/ fairfaxcountyvirginia/PST045218. Accessed January 2019.

U.S. Department of State. "Cold War History." https://www.history.com/topics/cold-war/cold-war-history Accessed January 2019.

U.S. Forest Service, "Science and Technology: Forest Health" https://www.fs.usda.gov/science-technology/ forest-health. Accessed January 2019.

Van Houten, Jennifer, Environmental Scientist. "Wetlands Studies and Solutions"; https://www.wetlands.com/; Conversations from June to September 2019.

Virginia Department of Forestry. "Forest Facts: Why We Need Trees" http://www.dof.virginia.gov/infopubs/_ forest-facts/FF-Why-We-Need-Trees_pub.pdf. Accessed October 2019.

Virginia Department of Historic Resources. https://www.dhr.virginia.gov/ Accessed September, 2018.

Virginia Department of Transportation. "A History of Roads in Virginia." www.virginiadot.org/about/resources/ historyofrds.pdf. Accessed October, 2018.

Waldman, Carl. *Atlas of the North American Indian*. 2000, New York, N.Y.: Checkmark Books, p. 36.

Weingroff, Richard. Agency Historian, Federal Highway Administration. Conversations from August to October 2019.

Welch, Deborah. *Virginia: An Illustrated History*. 2006. New York, New York: Hippocrene Books, p. 24.

"Wetlands Restoration Plan in Store for Huntley Meadows," *Alexandria Times*. August 16, 2007. https:// alextimes.com/2007/08/wetlands-restoration-plan-in-store-for-huntley-mea/ Accessed June 2019.

WetlandsWork Organization, "Benefits of Wetlands." https://www.wetlandswork.org/wetland-benefits. Accessed

June 2019.
Whitman, Julian. "Huntley Meadows Rescued by Community," *Mount Vernon Gazette*. September 9-15, 2010. Volume 21, Number 36. http://connectionarchives.com/PDF/2010/090810/Mt%20Vernon.pdf

Woodhouse, Henry. "Across the Atlantic Through the Air," *Dress and Vanity Fair*. 1913.

Woolley, Benjamin *Savage Kingdom: The True Story of Jamestown, 1607, and the Settlement of America*. 2007. New York, N.Y.: Harper Collins, p. 49.

Wren, Tony, P. *A Mason Family Country House*, 1971. Fairfax County Division of Planning under the direction of the County Board of Supervisors in cooperation with the County History Commission. Fairfax, Virginia. p. 41. Access provided through Project Gutenberg.

"Zeppelin," *Britannica online* encyclopedia. https://www.britannica.com/technology/zeppelin. Accessed November, 2018.

Acknowledgements

The process of putting this book together has been a joyful experience and I am grateful to the dedicated experts who have been generous with their time and assistance.

First, I am grateful to my wonderful wife, Candace, my muse who provided unfailing encouragement through this journey. I am indebted to Karen Sheffield, Park Manager, Carolyn Gamble, former Park Manager, and David Lawlor, Natural Resources Manager, leaders and consummate experts at Huntley Meadows Park. They generously provided valuable information making this project a pleasure. Thank you also to Elizabeth Train, Casey Pittrizzi, and the entire staff at the Norma Hoffman-Huntley Meadows Visitor Center, who helped with my many questions about the park.

Warmest thanks to Fred and Lisa Hoffman, husband and daughter of Norma Hoffman. They were most helpful providing background information and answering my questions about this remarkable leader.

Sincere thanks to Christopher Barbuschak, Virginia Room Librarian, at the Fairfax City Regional Library; Samantha Snyder, Reference Librarian and Angelica Yost, Assistant for Library Operations, both with the Fred W. Smith, National Library for the Study of George Washington, Historic Mount Vernon; and Samantha Dorsey, Curator of Collections, Historic Gunston Hall.

I appreciate the help of Angelina Callahan, Historian, United States Naval Research Laboratory; Richard Weingroff, Historian, Federal Highway Administration, U.S. Department of Transportation; Wendy Ormont, Program Leader, Federal Land to Parks Program, National Park Service; Patrick Kerwin, Manuscript Reference Librarian, Library of Congress; Heather Bollinger, Historic Records Manager, Fairfax Circuit Court Historic Records Center.; and Ryan Trainor, Archivist and Museum Specialist, the National Guard Memorial Library and Museum.

Kudos to Elizabeth Crowell, Archaeology and Collections Branch Manager, Fairfax County Park Authority; Jim Johnston, Author, and Historian; Christopher Bright, George Mason University Military Historian; Douglas Guiler, Army Veteran, International Affairs Expert and a great friend.

I am also grateful to Jennifer Van Houten, Environmental Scientist, Wetland Studies and Solutions; Daniel Schwartz, Soil Scientist, Northern Virginia Soil and Water Conservation District; Chris Sebastian, Public Affairs Coordinator, Duck's Unlimited; Harold Wood, Sierra Club; Charles V. Mauro, Civil War Historian; Thomas Thomas McAnear, Archivist, National Archives; Patricia Jollie, Museum Technician, Smithsonian Institution's National Museum of the American Indian; Aimee Wells, Archaeologist, Fairfax County Park Authority; Professor Danielle Moretti-Langholtz, Director, American Indian Resource Center, College of William and Mary; Kristen Sinclair, Ecologist, Fairfax County Park Authority; and Professor Kathryn Temple, Georgetown University. I am truly grateful to Alice Heiserman, whose expert editing and guidance has helped shape this book and to Xavaire Bolton, whose artistic eye brought my photographs to life.

I thank my mother, Diana Fisher, who introduced me to Alexandria, Virginia. On my first visit, I knew this would be home forever. Throughout her impressive career, which included working at Historic Mount Vernon and the White House Historical Association, she generously provided me access to national treasures such as the Mount Vernon estate and the White House.

About the Author

A native of Massachusetts, Rodney Fisher lives in Northern Virginia and regularly enjoys the tranquility of Huntley Meadows Park. The opportunity to experience some of the world's most beautiful places, as well as learning photography with his first camera (a fully manual, Fuji SLR), inspired his love of photography.

Mr. Fisher has served as a health care and education policy adviser for a member of the United States Senate. He also was a manager of federal governmental relations for a state education agency, leading the organization's Washington, D.C. office. An advanced Toastmaster, he has served as president of two clubs and has won three local contests in the Toastmasters International Speech competition. Mr. Fisher earned a bachelor's degree from the University of Mary Washington, and a master's degree from Georgetown University.

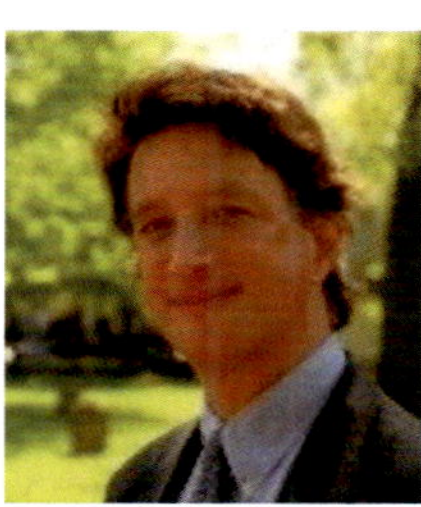